NAVIGATING T
FINANCIAL UNI

Author of the Ibis Press Bestsellers

Exploring the Financial Universe
Beginner's Guide to the Financial Universe

and

Money Signs
The Financial Universe

NAVIGATING
THE
FINANCIAL
UNIVERSE

Prospering and Preparing
for the Challenges Ahead

Christeen H. Skinner

Ibis Press
Lake Worth, FL

Published in 2019 by Ibis Press
A division of Nicolas-Hays, Inc.
P. O. Box 540206
Lake Worth, FL 33454-0206
www.ibispress.net

Distributed to the trade by
Red Wheel/Weiser, LLC
65 Parker St. • Ste. 7
Newburyport, MA 01950
www.redwheelweiser.com

Library of Congress Cataloging-in-Publication Data

Names: Skinner, Christeen, author.
Title: Navigating the financial universe : prospering and preparing for the
challenges ahead / Christeen H. Skinner.
Description: 1st [edition]. | Lake Worth, FL : Ibis Press,Inc., an imprint of
Nicolas Hays,Inc., 2019. | Includes bibliographical references.
Identifiers: LCCN 2019016827 | ISBN 9780892541898 (pbk. : alk. paper)
Subjects: LCSH: Astrology and personal finance. | Investments--Miscellanea.
Classification: LCC BF1729.F48 S555 2019 | DDC 133.5/83326--dc23
LC record available at https://lccn.loc.gov/2019016827

ISBN 978-0-89254-189-8
Ebook: ISBN 978-0-89254-684-8

Book design and production by Studio 31
www.studio31.com

[MV]
Printed in the United States of America

Dedication

To Michael

Contents

Appendices

Introduction

Elementary Rules of Navigation:

Financial Indicators and Rhythms in Your Chart

Before navigating the financial seas, it is wise to take stock of our position. We need to know what responsibilities and obligations echo from the past and what assets, if any, will fund us through the next stage of our financial journey.

What is now regarded as the "Global Financial Crisis" was front page news in 2008 but had, in fact, been building for many years before that. The quantitative easing used by some governments has made continued trade possible, but has not solved the real root: debt and its management. It is entirely possible that "Global Financial Crisis Part Two" waits in the wings, and that it will take as long to clear up the mess (whose roots lie in the 1980s) as it was to create it. The coming years— especially 2020–2028 will require careful thought.

Conditions, both financial and cosmic a decade and more since that earlier debacle, are now different; suggesting that fresh solutions will have to be found. Financial rocks and icebergs no doubt lie in wait requiring our look-outs (financial advisors) to be at their most observant. To be the best captain of your financial ship, however—and as only you know best your circumstances, attitudes and background—your personal navigational skills need to be in good working order. The aim of this book is to help you to achieve this.

In discussion with clients, I have observed that even those who successfully survived those still relatively-recent storms continue to have apprehension about the future. They sense, and in some cases know, that negotiating the next crisis will be every bit as demanding as that which was experienced in 2008.

Just as clients were alerted to the potential for that crisis in my first book *The Financial Universe* (2004), so in this book I propose to identify the time scale and arena of the next crisis. This work differs from earlier writing however in that within these chapters I explore ways of working with your own chart to strategize the best ways forward for the coming years.

Here I would like to be clear: this book is intended for anyone with even the vaguest of interest in our cosmic habitat, and the correlation between it and our financial lives. While I hope that experienced astrologers will be interested in my thoughts, my aim in this work is to reach out to those whose knowledge is still at "first aid" stage. If you understand how the year is divided into twelve signs of the zodiac—and know your personal sun or star sign—then I hope that you will find what follows interesting and useful.

Financial well-being IS important. The impact on physical health when we are burdened with debt or worry can have a devastating effect on life expectancy and enjoyment. "Future-proofing," so as to be able to fund lifespans that are now far longer than those of our parents or grandparents, presents new challenge. Old ways of working, earning, and saving no longer apply. Few are in positions where they can build—and rely upon—pension pots to sustain them adequately through what could be a prolonged "old age." It is likely that not only might individuals wish to work past the nominal retirement age of 65, but that this will be necessary—even essential. Planning for later life is now more important than ever.

Working with the rhythms of the stars and planets offers a unique perspective. I am of the opinion that adding knowledge and understanding of these cycles provides an extra tool to the trader's tool box and gives valuable assistance to investors of all kinds.

However, before beginning our journey and looking at the way ahead, we first need to appraise our cosmic habitat, our point of origin so to speak, and its probable influence on recent financial history.

Port of Origin

There are two "ports of origin" to consider: the collective and the personal. This section focuses on the apparent links between our position within the universe and present-day financial attitudes—the collective.

We start first with a long-term overview of the last thousand years and solar behavior.

You may be familiar with the term "retrograde." This is when, as observed from Earth, a planet appears to move in reverse direction. While this term is commonly used when discussing planet orbits, it might come as a surprise to learn that the term can also be used in relation to the Sun itself. The great "ball of fire" that is our Sun—and which appears to sit at the heart of our solar system—spins on its axis. This has a definite direction when considered against the *Barycenter*—the *actual* center of our solar system when the mass of the various planets is taken into consideration.

Approximately every 178 years— and with definite correlation to the cycles of Jupiter, Saturn, Uranus, and Neptune—the Sun appears to spin in the opposite direction. This last occurred in April 1990—not many months after the fall of the Berlin Wall. What followed this event was the equivalent of an economic earthquake.

A review of meteorological history reveals that in the years following a solar retrograde, there is disturbance to terrestrial weather systems. This, of course, affects growing systems. Governments cannot control the weather. However, it can be shown that political decisions taken in these post retrograde periods have led to instability, war, and, frequently, economic challenge.

The terrestrial climate of post-solar-retrograde periods has proved severe. Ocean currents are affected and an increase in earth movements (earthquakes and volcanoes) occurs. Volcanic eruption offers a particular type of disturbance to human activity in that the debris thrown into the atmosphere has the potential to obliterate sunshine—devastating crops and threatening all life. In each earlier and recorded instance, commerce has been affected. New trading routes have had to be found. Prosperous areas have become less so and areas of previous poverty thrived in changed conditions.

In the last thousand years, five solar retrogrades have been recorded: in the thirteenth century (The Wolf Minimum), the late fifteenth century (Sporer Minimum), the late seventeenth century (Maunder Minimum), the late eighteenth century (Dalton Minimum) and, more recently, an, as yet, unnamed minimum in the late twentieth century.

The suggested length of the Wolf Minimum was fifty years. This covered the period of the Black Death and much of the Hundred Years War between the French and English.

Civil war in both England (the Wars of the Roses) and Spain followed the second instance, the Sporer Minimum.

The Maunder Minimum (or the Little Ice Age) coincided with the overthrow of the Ming Dynasty in China, uprisings in Japan, civil war again in England and, in Germany, the Thirty Years' war.

Next came the Dalton Minimum which coincided with the French Revolution and the American Civil War. The Dalton Minimum may also have been a factor in determining the outcome of the battle of Waterloo in June 1815. The battle was affected by an unusual major weather system. Dust in the atmosphere, created by the eruption of Mount Tambora in Indonesia two months earlier, delayed the start of the battle. This eruption was yet another factor in contributing to a fall in global temperatures by three degrees Fahrenheit.

The Sun's most recent retrograde—which may mark the as yet unnamed fifth minimum—began in April 1990, when Saturn, Uranus and Neptune were all grouped on one side of the Sun while gigantic Jupiter was at the other. This period saw the collapse of the USSR and the emergence of several new states. At the geological level, since this most recent retrograde, the world has seen increased volcanic activity—the most famous of which was the eruption of the Icelandic volcano which brought air traffic to a standstill in February 2007.

I suspect that the effect of this most recent retrograde is yet to be fully experienced. What we have seen already are large movements of people such as mass migrations from Sub-Sahara into Europe. And we can easily recognize the accompanying political instability. Further evidence of mass movement is evident in the USA where more and more people are choosing to leave northern states for better climes and tax structures, let alone the problems along the US southern border.

The Far East (China) will surely also be affected. With more and more people inhabiting their cities—and deserts encroaching on these—sustaining life threatens to be major issue across vast swathes of Asia. Again we should expect to see mass migration south.

Perhaps the most obvious evidence of present-day political instability are the war and mass migration in the Middle East. The First Gulf War began not too long after the solar retrograde. If history repeats, then we may only be a third or half the way through the period of war in those regions. Even without the terrors of war, there may be very good reason for families to leave this area of the Earth. Climatic change could render vast areas of the Mideast almost uninhabitable.

As you will read, taking into account the sun-spot rhythm and the expected low in 2019–2020, we probably have a long way to go in this latest sun-retrograde.

In my original *Financial Universe,* a chapter was entitled "Water Wars." My conclusion then was that from 2010 on, lack of available water supply would lead to both war and migration. Thus far, the basic human need for water has been obscured by wars based on religious fundamentalism. Satellite imagery though shows that the two main sources of water in the Mideast—the Euphrates and Tigris—are not flowing as they have in the past. This gives rise to irrigation difficulties and will lead to diminished harvests. This will also probably not be the only part of the world affected by water shortage. Variations on this theme are likely around the Nile and Yangtse deltas and across many of the world's major rivers.

This should be of deepening concern to all. Concentration of human life into increasingly densely populated cities raises the potential for pandemics.

Water may yet be the new gold. Before going any further in this work, I would urge investors to consider companies providing clean water services, transportation and security for water, and even the purchase of land with the potential to provide this life-giver. True, even then there are no guarantees. Supplies could be contaminated—again suggesting that security will be a fast-growing sector in the coming years.

Much, much more could be written on the topic of the solar retrograde and the impact it has had and could yet have on human life and behavior. For now it is sufficient to recognize that we are in the midst of a period which has, in the past, brought enormous change to the geopolitical world and which is likely to continue to do for some years to come. Borders are likely to change, new countries form, and fresh trade agreements be needed. All this will be explored further in a later chapter.

Clearly then, our asset management will require a very different kind of care to that demanded of our most recent ancestors: neither your parents, grandparents, nor their parents have lived through the type of stormy financial seas that lie in wait.

We live in exciting times and have greater knowledge than ever about what lies beyond our solar system. While so many light years distant from us, where our solar system is in relation to points in deep space is relevant. Astro-economic history suggests a resonance between our solar system alignments with these far distant points and human behaviour—and, from the perspective of this work, clear correlation with economic activity.

The Galactic Center

Our solar system is one of many in the galaxy known as the Milky Way. Thousands if not millions of stars are held within this system by a complex gravitational pull emanating from an apparently super-massive Black Hole at its center. A massive power source emanating strong radio waves is found near this degree suggesting a high concentration of radio-active energy. Relative to the stars, the Galactic Center advances approximately seventy-two minutes (a little over a degree) per century. At the start of the twenty-first century it had arrived at 27 Sagittarius.

The power of this energy source is considerable. A myriad

of star-systems revolve around it: held in position millions and millions of light years from it. The range of its influence is truly extraordinary.

It should come as no surprise that as planets in our own solar system align with the Galactic Center, that this coincides with "eventfulness" here on Earth. The Sun aligns with the Galactic Center a few days before the December solstice each year. Those born around this date do indeed seem to have a life force that often results in them being marked out as "special."

Though the transit of the Sun across this degree should not be confused with the relatively common "end of year" rally, it is interesting that it is common for stocks to rise between December 17 (when the Sun approaches the Galactic Center) and the December solstice.

As viewed from Earth, Mercury and Venus pass this degree at least once annually—occasionally more than once if either planet has a retrograde period near this degree. Mars aligns with the Galactic Center at least once every couple of years (again more than once if a retrograde period is involved) while Jupiter aligns with this area of the zodiac every dozen or so years. It is interesting that since 2007, in the days following Mars' conjunction with the Galactic centre, that the Standard & Poor Index (SPX) has lost value. Jupiter last aligned with this degree in 2007. In the weeks following this alignment, the SPX fell markedly.

The Galactic Center (GC) is a point of moving energy, and it is appropriate to allow for a small "orb" or period of radiance. It is equivocally not possible for us to say that Saturn, for example, will be at exactly this point on a certain date. The slower-moving the planet, the longer it will take the planet to pass the Galactic Center and the area of influence around it. To traders this is exasperating—although the crossing heralds tantalizingly promising big moves, the actual date is elusive. However, the fact that a period of weeks or months can be identified as prone to certain types of action, is useful information. Through study of other cycles, greater clarity (and opportunities!) can be gleaned.

In 2007—and slightly ahead of the global financial crisis—Pluto aligned with this degree of the Galactic Center. Pluto is associated with the underworld. As the number of sub-prime loans escalated during that year, the stage was being set for the financial traumas to come in the following year. Pluto's orbit is approximately 246 years, so that it aligns with the Galactic Center four times in every millennium. However, though Pluto will not pass the Galactic Center for another two and a half centuries, we should not conclude that a variation on the 2007 global crash will not occur within our lifetimes.

As we now know, the entire global financial system—and more than one government—were brought to near collapse as Pluto made alignment with the Galactic Center and then made its Capricorn ingress. (Capricorn is the sign associated with large institutions, corporations, and governments.) Stability in these large institutions is thus unlikely until after Pluto leaves Capricorn in 2024. Between now and then, we should be prepared for the possibility of another debt crisis—with the potential to once again bring the global financial system to near collapse.

Fractures, if not definite collapse, may well appear as other planets make aspect to the Galactic Center. You will find a list of potentially red-letter key dates in Appendix 1.

ALERTS AHEAD

Solar Activity, Black Holes, the Galactic Center, and the Super Galactic Center

Here are a series of patterns and cosmic events to come over the next decade that are of interest to every reader, their friends, and families. All four of these are expanded upon throughout this book. These alerts include the probable solar effects, activity, degree position, relation to black holes, the Galactic Center, and the Super Galactic Center. We list areas of concern that will help both citizens and traders through some of the rough seas ahead.

First Alert (Solar Activity)

The next expected sun-spot minimum (2019) may have already occurred before you started reading this. In 2019, the Moon, whose distance from Earth varies, also reached its closest point to Earth as part of a nineteen-year cycle. When these two cycles (sunspot minima and Moon perigee) have coincided in the past, the effect on terrestrial weather systems was catastrophic. Crop prices rose as crops became scarce through failure to grow, or through drought or, in some parts of the world, were demolished by driving rains. History shows that these minima and lunar perigee conditions occurred a century ago when Australia experienced one of its worst droughts ever. In 2018 there were already signs of a repetition. It is probable that recovery will not occur until at least 2021.

Advances in storage techniques have resulted in many people in the world being oblivious to the effect of weather on food supplies. However, possible drought, disturbed weather patterns, and strong earth movement (quakes, volcanic activity etc.) will drive the message home that humankind is vulnerable to much that is beyond our control. While this is a disturbing scenario, it could also be seen as opportunity for those able to offer good and reliable storage and distribution facilities. The latter, however, may be vulnerable to cosmic activity that renders this difficult to achieve on anything other than a local scale (see below).

While the impact on crop growing at solar minima combined with lunar position will likely be hugely significant, of no less importance is the probability of other disasters; attributable to either disturbed solar behavior or other cosmic events. Such disasters will be unlike any other in recorded history simply because they affect business enterprises that were unheard of in earlier times.

As we know, the planets are held in orbit by the gravitational pull of the Sun. It could also be said that the planets have impact on solar activity, i.e., there is an inter-connection. When planets are grouped together on one side of the Sun, it appears that solar flares and coronal mass ejections (CMEs) are more likely. The potential for one of these solar events to knock out satellite systems and so disrupt distribution networks is increased. It is doubtless already on the minds of many working in this field to find ways to protect—if possible—this kind of equipment from cosmic sabotage.

We are used to crops grown on one side of the world appearing on super-market shelves on the other side of the world just a few days later. With accurate data recording, many firms know exactly when and where to aim their supplies. Suppose a solar flare were to knock out a satellite system? Depots could struggle to receive or deliver goods.

Nor should we ignore the possibility of cosmic forces emanating from elsewhere in the solar system affecting life systems. There is already conjecture of a possible link between increased incidence of cardiac arrest and "killer electrons" reaching Earth from the Van Allen Belt. Clearly what is going on outside the Earth's atmosphere is every bit as important as what is happening within it. Greater understanding of the impact and, perhaps the ability to forecast these disturbances, has implications for the health industry (and possibly for investors).

To repeat, we should be in no doubt as to the increasing importance of satellite systems—which are surely vulnerable to disturbance via solar wind or other cosmic ray particles. With every "advance" in technical systems—on which food distribution systems, GPS systems, "intelligent fridges," and banking networks now operate—the risk of chaos should there be a breakdown or interference in the operation of such communication infrastructure exponentially grows.

So what is the likelihood of solar behavior disturbing these systems? It is possible to forecast solar flux and solar radio activity—but only about 27 days in advance. You can find out more about potentially disturbing solar activity via _www.spaceweather. com_.

As mentioned, the distribution of the planets around our special star is important too. Through 2019 and 2020, several planets are grouped on one side of the Sun. The "pull" or "draw" of these positions could have serious effect on our central star. This arrangement of the planets is rare. Certainly we have not experienced quite like this in our lifetimes. Indeed, it's necessary to go back to the late thirteenth century to find anything remotely similar. Since there were no electronic market trading systems in operation at that time, we cannot compare like with like. That said, what we do know of the late thirteenth century is that this was a very difficult period for banking—with many collapsing through unpaid debts! Perhaps the past will repeat.

Focusing purely on solar behavior though, we can say that is that within the last century it has been known for coronal mass ejections (CMEs) to knock out electrical systems and, on occasion, affect entire cities. This is something for which we should all be prepared. (Arguably one of the best investments will be to have good friends and neighbors as well, of course, as candles and other essentials at the ready!)

Second Alert: 19° Capricorn and the Black Hole

In my earlier work *Exploring the Financial Universe* (2016), I examined stock market "crashes" of the twentieth century showing that in each and every case, 19 degree of a Cardinal signs (Aries, Cancer, Libra or—especially, Capricorn) was involved.

Nineteen degrees Capricorn is, in fact, the degree area of a black hole. This black hole emits a different energy to that found at the Galactic Center but is of no lesser importance. We should also note that 19 Capricorn is the position of Pluto's South Node: the degree at which Pluto crosses the ecliptic (the Sun's apparent path around Earth).

Whether it is the former or the latter that is the coincidental factor in equities losing value, the fact remains that transits over this degree have, in the past, coincided with market moves to the negative. There is little reason to think that this response to planetary alignment with this area of the zodiac will change.

(Through much of 2018 and 2019, Pluto will pass through 19 Capricorn. As Pluto is a slow-moving planet, determining the actual date when losses might be incurred requires further study.)

Nor should we omit Jupiter from our studies. Jupiter aligns with the Galactic Center is 2019. At both this crossing and as Jupiter reaches 19 Capricorn in 2020 exaggerated or strong market moves are to be expected.

Third Alert: Super Galactic Center

The alignment of Saturn and Neptune with the Super Galactic Center will be covered in depth in a later chapter. For now, please note that this alignment, in 2026, coincides with a probable global recession. It will surely be vital for all to have a financial safety net in place well ahead of this "comic appointment."

Fourth Alert: Nodal or Business Cycle

We should not leave this primary analysis of our present position without giving consideration to the NODAL—OR BUSINESS CYCLE, an equally important consideration to the others.

It was noted by the financial astrologer Louise McWhirter, that there was correlation between the accepted 20 year business cycle and the lunar nodal cycle (in fact 18.6 years in length). The lunar node moves backwards through the zodiac. As it moves from Aquarius to Leo, the cycle tends upward, whereas from Leo to Aquarius it turns down.

Since that earlier work was written, the lunar node has made five complete cycles—each following this same trend with the value of stocks moving quickly higher as the Node passes from Scorpio to Leo, plateauing as the Node moves through Cancer and then declining until the Node reaches Aquarius when the cycle begins anew.

The lunar node leaves Leo for Cancer in late 2018 by which time a downturn should be obvious. If the past repeats as suggested by this cycle, we should not anticipate an upturn until the Node arrives in Aquarius in 2027.

This alert is most important. Since 2007 (when the Node was in Aquarius) the value of stocks has soared despite the low having coincided with the Global Financial Crash. Few would surely have expected that the Dow Jones Index would soar above 20,000 after that earlier debacle. True, there has not been a constant upward trajectory and there has been volatility along the way. Even so, many indices have reached quite unexpected levels. It is quite possible that some investors may have been lured into thinking that this trend will continue.

That is unlikely to be the case; suggesting that those retiring in the coming years will need to brace themselves for investments yielding much reduced reward.

The Nodal cycle is intricately linked with eclipse cycles. Eclipses—which may be thought of as "cosmic punctuation marks"—require careful negotiation. In another chapter we will assess what helpful hints can be gained from foreknowledge of their position in the zodiac and the land areas over which they are observed.

Over-Arching Cycles and a Final Alert—or Food for Thought

The two planets, Pluto and Neptune respectively take 246 and 148 years to complete one circuit of the zodiac. These two planets align (form a conjunction) every half-millennium. If we look back on the last few thousand years, we find that these conjunctions have coincided with trading emphasis moving from East to West hemisphere and back again.

Their most recent conjunction was in the late nineteenth century. Though this is arguably too simplistic a statement, the move from West-hemisphere trading domination to East-hemisphere can broadly be recognized. There is likely yet more to come so that investors should now be on the look-out for opportunities across East Asia.

No less important is the Southern hemisphere. Though the shift from West to East and back again is not as noticeable, a North-South cycle of alternating 500 year (Neptune-Pluto cycle) phases can be discerned. Later in this work we will look at opportunities to invest in both Latin America and in Africa.

The most recent Neptune-Pluto cycle began in the sign of Gemini. This will be the case for the next four such cycles. The starting point moves along by approximately 10 degrees each time.

Few would disagree that advances in communications and related technology have driven stock markets higher since 1891. These same sectors will surely have great impact in the coming years too. Certainly this is a key sector where there should be opportunities for reward.

Perhaps no less important will be transport. Just as the early part of the twentieth century saw expansion in rail networks, so the coming years could bring great investment (and later, profit) in infrastructure projects.

Developments in these areas—and specifically where the companies are registered in the East—are probable and should provide promising returns.

As with all planets, elliptical orbits result in them spending longer in some signs than in others. Rarely do the two change signs in the same year. In 2024, Pluto will move from Capricorn to Aquarius while a year later, Neptune moves from Pisces to Aries.

It is probable then that the years 2024 (Pluto's Aquarius ingress) through to 2027 (the expected recession) will witness profound developments in financial activity at all levels.

Our Position

In taking stock of our position then, we can surely all agree that our financial boats, though they appear to have managed to remain afloat through recent storms, have yet to be tested against the cosmic weather patterns now on the horizon. While we can do little to mitigate these, we do now have an understanding of potential dangers.

Next on our "to do" list is to consider our financial engine and how it can be maintained.

The Need for a Financial Engine Check

Before leaving harbor, it is wise to check the state of your financial engine, and your attitude to finance and functioning. It may be that these are overdue for maintenance.

First though, let's be clear: somewhere within every chart there is a degree of financial acumen. It just has to be found. This is an exercise that can be done either on your own, or with assistance from a financial advisor or a professional astrologer, and preferably both.

It is curious that although most people go for regular health checks and that most also understand the basic concepts of hygiene and diet needed to maintain well-being, so few people give real attention to their financial health. There are, of course, many reasons for this: not least of which is that these routines and skills are rarely taught in schools.

Often financial attitudes are copied from parents who themselves may not be particularly well educated in this area. As you become familiar with planetary cycles you may well wish to review the position of the planets at your parents' and even grandparents' births to understand familial habits better. These are important legacies.

When working closely with trading or investment-orientated clients on financial matters, I am keen to learn about any early experiences of handling money and of buying and selling. As far as I can tell, those who gain experience before they leave school tend to have better financial health than those whose experiences came much later.

In particular, when working with traders, it is helpful to identify times when they have enjoyed success. Reviewing the planetary conditions under which positive events occurred is extremely helpful. Armed with this information, it becomes possible to plan and prepare for potentially favorable future periods. The same is true, of course, for periods when traders have "lost" (though it could be argued that these apparent failures were master classes in how NOT to trade).

This book is intended for everyone. Therefore, we cannot possibly address the myriad of possibilities that might be considered. Every chart (horoscope) is unique. In addition, your financial "engine" is yours alone. It may be under or even overused, but either way it is special to you. While this work cannot offer an interpretation of your personal horoscope, it can, I hope, say something about the strategies available to assist your particular financial needs and goals.

Please note that there is no singular planetary picture that decrees you will be rich or poor. What is evident in all lives is that there are financial rhythms: tides that are slow turning and at other times, tides which turn so fast there is barely time to launch the lifeboat. To prepare for either, your personal chart (with exact time, date, and place of birth) needs to be studied. That said, there are a few generalizations that can be made:

A Word on Pluto

Most people accept that there are differences between generations. These age-definitions give context: a framework through which we understand the nuances of a period of time. What follows works on this principle: defining groups of births by the position of a single and important member of our solar system, Pluto.

In examining our financial engines, assessment of Pluto's position and status has proved a valuable exercise. It might seem absurd that a small orbiting rock at huge distance from Earth could have impact on our lives in any way. Yet study of horoscopes, and comparison with major events, suggests more than a tenuous link. It is also true that the inter-connection between Pluto's position and other planets in a chart varies hugely from one individual to another. Such data would be considered carefully when looking at a personal chart. Even without an individualized review however, it is possible to draw conclusions from the position of Pluto by sign in a chart. Pluto moves slowly: spending years in one sign before moving to the next. Its position by sign or sector of the zodiac yields invaluable information as to the tendencies and attitudes of large groups of people.

If you have your birth chart but are, as yet, are unfamiliar with the length of planet cycles you may be amused to know that by telling an astrologer that you were born with *e.g.,* Pluto in Leo, you are also telling them that you were born between (approximately) 1939 and 1956. The more experienced the astrologer, the better able they are to mentally calculate your chart, or conversely, to know from a given planet position, when you were born. Astrologers understand generations and behavioral patterns through their knowledge of slow-moving planet cycles.

Pluto is the planet associated with regeneration and renewal: it is the dark oil, or the battery pack of your financial engine. These are good analogies in that we all know that oil and oil filters need to be changed frequently for an engine to run smoothly. We also know that batteries are drained through use and that they eventually require recharging. Again, the precise time-period between oil change or the recharging of batteries varies from person to person and requires interpretation by an experienced professional astrologer who has access to the whole chart. Yet, broad outlines using Pluto's position by sign can be given.

This is useful information for financial advisors. By understanding the needs and desires of different generations, it should be possible to build portfolios based on the individual's strengths and interests, as well as to identify areas and periods of potential weakness.

Pluto Generations

There are six distinct "Pluto" groups alive today. The financial history of each of these Pluto planet periods also offers an under-standing of the pressures that parents and grandparents of these distinct generational groups experienced during an individual's childhood. Tensions and occasionally memorable events will have left their mark.

Our elders' attitude to financial affairs provides a role model that we later emulate or reject. In understanding the financial background that we absorbed as children, we can learn much about our attitudes and how we have sought to overcome negative aspects while enhancing positive ones.

- Group One covers the period between 1939 and 1956 as Pluto moved through Leo, including an unusual group born between 1956 and 1957.
- Group Two: covers 1957 to 1971 with Pluto in Virgo. It includes the mid 60s which, as we will see, brought profound change not just at the political and social level, but at the economic level also.
- Group Three: 1972 to 1983, Pluto in Libra
- Group Four: covers 1984 through 1995, Pluto in Scorpio
- Group Five: covers 1995 to 2008, Pluto in Sagittarius
- And Group Six: 2008 through 2024, Pluto in Capricorn

(Precise dates of sign change are given in Appendix 2.)

To be clear, each of these groups has its own financial operating system. Some need frequent oil or filter changes, while others hold their battery charge longer or recharge at a faster rate than others.

We must also note that as Pluto concludes its stay in one sign—and before crossing into the next—ripples have occurred across the financial world as new currents generated by Pluto's pending sign changes are felt. Each Pluto generation is faced with learning new financial instruments and services that were not available to earlier generations.

Though the coming years promise new—and perhaps even as yet unimaginable challenges—it should be remembered that just as other generations negotiated difficulties, we too will likely do the same.

Financial Rapids Ahead

In 2023, Pluto will cross from Capricorn into Aquarius, and in 2036, from that sign into Pisces. The move from one sign to another is referred to in astrology as an "ingress." Throughout history, ingresses made by the slow-moving planets (e.g. Uranus, Neptune and Pluto) have coincided with seismic developments on the global financial stage.

The fact that the next Pluto ingress coincides within the space of a few months with Neptune's Aries ingress and with Uranus' Gemini ingress, suggests that 2023–2026 will bring a series of heavy-duty challenges. No sooner will we have coped with one financial turmoil than the next will be upon us. While hopefully we won't need to make use of lifeboats, we will surely need to know where they are.

Whether or not we are ship-wrecked by what will surely be fast-paced developments will depend not just on our ability to negotiate the changes that lie ahead, but also the state of our financial engines.

What follows are notes on each of the Pluto generations, and how you might consider preparing for the journey ahead.

GROUP ONE:
The Pluto in Leo Generation: 1939–1956

For the parents of those with Pluto in Leo, budgeting was part and parcel of their everyday lives. Though the rationing of the World War II years was over by the end of this period, those with Pluto in Leo grew up watching their parents "making do and mending." They were also doubtless aware of how their parents saved, when possible, and how they treasured their nest eggs. It was not abnormal for their parents to bank where their own parents had banked. They may never even have thought of doing things differently. Thus many of the Pluto in Leo generation "inherited" loyalty to a particular bank: a loyalty that was later found to be ill-deserved.

Like their parents, those with Pluto in Leo (Group One) did not have immediate access to the numerous credit facilities available today. Early banking relationships were built on passbooks: documents which showed exactly how much was deposited, saved, and spent. This "black and white" financial system put focus on interest charged and gained. Many "inherited" a deference to bankers and rarely questioned where their savings were invested: questions that would be raised when Pluto reached the next of the Fire signs, Sagittarius, between 1995 and 2008.

As children, those with Pluto in Leo witnessed their elders go from making do with little, to delight in restraints being removed. Such was their pleasure at having, for example, a first brand new coat made with fresh material and to a customized style. These children were no doubt given the impression that "brand new" was best.

It is not at all surprising that those with Pluto in Leo are tempted by new styles and ideas and less enthralled by the idea of repurposing items. Although, since Pluto entered Capricorn, that idea has become more attractive.

As explained at the start of this chapter, ahead of Pluto's move from one sign to another there has always been a recognizable and significant development in the financial world. In the USA, Fannie Mae, the Federal National Mortgage Association, came into being a few months *before* Pluto entered Leo. This prepared Group One for the prospect of living better than earlier generations, even while paying off the debt (as opposed to saving the whole amount needed first). Fannie Mae was licensed to issue bonds and to use the proceeds to buy mortgages from local Savings and Loans organizations. The latter were prohibited from lending to borrowers living more than 50 miles from their offices. With the launch of Fannie Me, home loans became affordable and home ownership in the US increased substantially. An important point to note is that generally the lender knew the person to whom they were lending and, through this connection, had a fair idea of the person's circumstances, and as a result had confidence that the debt would be honored and repaid.

Similarly, on the other side of the Atlantic, in the United Kingdom, there was also emphasis on housing. Initially, post-war impetus was on social housing, but by the by 50s, privately built homes were on the increase. The number of mortgage lenders was growing. Home ownership became something to which many aspired—even if that aspiration meant incurring debt to which their grandparents would not have had access.

It is not hard to imagine the pride of those early mortgagees as they stepped onto the housing ladder. The influence this had on their children was surely considerable. Even now—and despite the many ups and downs that housing markets have experienced in the last half century—when questioned as to what is best "Pension or Property?" many of those with Pluto in Leo respond with the latter. Indeed, for a significant number, the idea of owning more than one home is an aim if not a realization.

Homes back in the late 50s and 60s tended to be uncluttered. People simply did not have all the possessions now deemed essential. Time and again, when discussing financial matters with clients who grew up during these years, I am struck by references to how they now feel to have "too much" and need to "declutter." Most recognize that through much of their adult years they have needed to own more, but that with so many non-essential items, they feel they have clogged up their lives. Many of these people are now declaring the intention to take action to declutter: in the process boosting coffers through the sale of no-longer-needed items.

This earlier expenditure is understandable: with the advent of the concept of buying items "over time," and then credit cards, those with Pluto in the Fire sign Leo have rarely had to wait long to own a product or buy a service. Indeed, for many, instant gratification has been possible. Their financial engines have been oiled by lines of extended credit and even now, beyond retirement age, by the possibility of equity release.

Looking Ahead

How this group will cope with the challenges of the coming decade will obviously vary from person to person. It is likely that those who are unable to find new lines of credit will find the coming years very hard indeed. Very few are likely to be in the fortunate position of holding large pension pots able to sustain them through the coming years. We now know that many of this generation will live far beyond the recognized retirement age of 65—possibly even for thirty or more years.

Many of these individuals will experience Pluto traveling

through Leo's opposite sign of Aquarius (2024–2040). Unless they are in the fortunate position to be able to self-fund retirement, they will likely need to adopt a more Aquarian way of living: pooling resources, sharing with like-minded people, and forming co-operatives. The very thought of this might be anathema as Pluto makes its way through Capricorn. This group could yet surprise themselves by discovering latent childhood talents for thrift, creativity and purpose, and a willingness to join forces for the common good. Indeed, they may delight within these groups in showing skills and talents that have long been buried. By bringing their ships together, they may hope to be better protected from the storms ahead.

While the coming years will need to be navigated with particular care, it is worth noting that between 2026 and 2028, Uranus (the planet associated with entrepreneurship) will be just a third of a cycle from Pluto, and have moved into Gemini. This is one of the focused communication zones of the zodiac. This phase will likely find the Pluto in Leo generation rising to the challenge of that age by banding together, comparing notes, supporting creativity, and improving their financial situations through cooperation and association.

Leo is a Fire sign and as we know, can go from a dying ember to a raging forest fire: it is both dangerous and useful. The generation with Pluto in Leo often displays a tendency to go from one financial extreme to another. They can show extraordinary creativity and reap financial reward as a result. Yet they may also roar that they have "nothing" and are cash-strapped, while at other times acting as though they have money to burn. Unlike their parents and grandparents, few are quiet about their financial position; often validating their behavior with their circumstances. They will scream that they "positively cannot do without" a certain thing or service, while an onlooker may think not only that they can but that they should.

That same onlooker may be amazed by the occasionally breath-taking audacity of someone with Pluto in Leo as he or she launches a new enterprise. Rarely is this done quietly: there is, whenever Leo is involved, a need for theater and audience. This group loves the launch, the razzamatazz, the packaging, and, of course, the attention.

Even those not inspired to start up their own enterprise seem to have a need to leave others with distinct impression of their resources. Though quite uncomfortable—ashamed even—if they have insufficient cash to take part in some adventure or other, they rarely dampen the enthusiasm of others. Perhaps more than any other generational group, these people understand that goodwill and loyalty is as important as firm capital.

Those from other generations (parents, children or financial advisors) draw the conclusion that what this group needs is better control! They deduce that with better self-regulation, this group could be saved from lurching from crisis to crisis.

This view though arguably misses the point of the very special qualities of these people—a readiness to let their creativity take flight, and invest in themselves and their ideas. Many from this generation have brought new businesses to market, both during their early working lives and post the usual "retirement" age of 65. It seems to be a thrill they need to experience in their lives. True, some have taken risks of a certain magnitude. Nor have these ventures necessarily been driven by a need to make money: it is as likely that passion has been the driver.

My experience with clients shows that many of these individuals have experience of quite awesome financial escapades: the equivalent of high-wire acts. Certainly one or two have taken my breath away with tales involving levels of risk that are anathema to me—even though I too come from this generation. So much depends on the personal chart.

Only recently did it dawn on me that few of these individuals ever spoke of financial advisors or mentors. They would look almost quizzical at the suggestion. Unlike their immediate forebears, for whom saving and thrift were central to their financial approach, and who regularly met with their bank manager or advisor for annual assessment of their financial picture, my experience of those with Pluto in Leo is that they have shied away from this regular monitoring with others and relied rather more on their own ability to maintain control—not always with success!

It should be noted, as mentioned earlier, that this generation was the first to have relatively easy access to credit. Needs and desires could be quickly met with the result that many with Pluto in this sector of the zodiac have difficulty in applying the self-discipline to save.

Of course, amongst this group are those who did build substantial pension nest-eggs. This often happened by default however: the money was collected from pay-packets and invested on their behalf. The actual running of these funds was done at some distance, so that they did not have direct involvement. Very few have operated their own schemes. In short, many have financial engines that haven't been well-maintained at the personal level but they have profited from the diligence of others.

One of the very interesting features of recent times has been the intense analysis of people's spending habits when they apply for mortgages. True, this is an understandable legacy of the subprime mortgage crisis. Note that some of those now running today's banks were born between 1939 and 1956. They may be correct in deducing that controls need to be applied, but they are probably applying these "rules" to the wrong generation! They may wish that such attention had been paid to their spending habits: a case of the pot calling the kettle black. Those born later, and with Pluto in Virgo, Libra, or Scorpio are unlikely to need this kind of scrutiny.

The Leo financial engine is often not sufficiently well maintained. They may not, for example, do a full risk assessment before moving off on yet another financial adventure. Often these individuals get their fingers burned: a few have no difficulty at all in recalling financial "incidents" between 1995 and 2008, when Pluto passed through another of the Fire signs, Sagittarius. Reflection often leads them to thinking they made errors of judgement. Actually, they may simply have been too hasty and raced into schemes promising reward, but which came unstuck when they didn't get "out" at the right time. It is rather easier for this group to jump into a scheme than to get out of it.

This generation, either retired or almost retired, may hopefully be wiser. But many have growing and understandable concern as to how they will cope in their later years. Bearing in mind that Pluto enters the opposite sign to Leo, Aquarius, in 2023, and that many from this generation are likely to live through Pluto's transit of this sign, their fears are likely justified. A common financial weakness for this group is coming to the sudden realization that action is needed, and rush to right their situation—often giving in to their tendency to go for quick fix.

Pluto in Leo Service Record

A good engine also has a good service record. In planning for the next stage of their financial lives, those with Pluto in Leo (a Fixed sign), may find it useful to review their—even if desultory—financial service records for the period 1984–1995 when Pluto passed through the next in the sequence of Fixed signs, Scorpio. As you might expect, there is a very big difference between Fire sign Leo and Water sign Scorpio, even if they share attributes of determination, resistance, and loyalty. Leo may be theatrical and obvious in its action while a Scorpio trait is stealth. Indeed, it is entirely possible that even now, those born with Pluto in Leo have yet to realize the value of experiences (not just investments) made as Pluto moved through the latter sign. Taking time to work through the financial adventures of 1984–1995 and listing connections and investments made during that period may yet prove valuable to the Leo group. Though the cosmos does not "do repeats," there is likely much to learn ahead of Pluto's move into the NEXT Fixed sign, Aquarius, in 2023.

It is unlikely that each of the years 1984–1995 were all "bad" or all "good" financially. What is likely is that that those with Pluto in Leo experienced the need to apply obvious thrift. Recall that interest rates soared through this period—which may well have been a driver. Even so, they may also have spent cash that they felt to have been essential at the time (children's education, bricks and mortar, etc.) and where that investment was unquantifiable. Few could have known how the value of property would soar.

My experience is that many from this group are already in a state of panic about their financial future. The very idea of "just managing" is intolerable. Many have no idea how they would cope if forced to live in uncongenial environment and without certain luxuries.

Most are at the stage of fearing inability to conserve resources. They should not, however, underplay their undoubted entrepreneurial capabilities. Many have skills, talents and experiences that could yet either form a revenue stream or give them bargaining power. Obviously this cannot be true for all, but neither should this potential be ignored.

Of paramount importance to the Pluto in Leo generation will be to have a good network of friends in place prior to Pluto's arrival in Aquarius. Whereas earlier generations could count on family structures to sustain them to end of life, it is probable that this particular generation will need friends to act as family. Investing in friendships should be viewed as a top priority. Shared understanding of the predicaments and vagaries of dealing with declining health gives extra premium to the value of the unconditional love and support offered by networks of friends and neighbors.

There is a most interesting period before Pluto arrives in Leo's opposite, Aquarius, when both Jupiter and Saturn pass through the latter sign together. Though attention would, of course, need to be given to the personal chart, for the better part of a year following the December solstice in 2020, focusing on that extra funding source should not prove too onerous and might well provide a useful revenue stream.

It is during 2021 too that these individuals will discover the value of being part of a group: not least for the discounts bulk-buying can bring, but also because by then they will likely be acutely aware that connections—and friendships—have great value.

Immediate advice to the Leo generation is—and of course this is obvious—focus on maximizing health, ensure a good network on whom you can rely, attend to any urgent domestic repairs, and lastly, set aside a day to assess both your financial position and real needs. If it's been a long time since you checked on basic facts: house insurance costs, etc., then listing these is imperative.

Of course this has nothing to do with the position of the planets. But knowing these liabilities is essential before embarking on the next stage of your financial journey.

Maintaining the Pluto in Leo Financial Engine

Some years ago I hit upon a thought when working with a client with Pluto in Leo who had her own successful business. She has no intention of retiring as such but was beginning to show concern for future needs. In discussion it became clear that the financial management of her company was left very much to her accountant, while she focuses on the creative side. When asked simple questions about the cost of her car insurance or mobile phone contract, she was unsure. There was no problem in paying these bills, but clearly it had been a long time since these contracts were reviewed.

We came up with a plan: just as her company had an "end of year" when the income and expenses of the previous year were calculated and tax liabilities deduced, that we would choose another date for her personal annual review. This was not to be confused with her tax year. Nor would this take the form of a standard profit and loss statement. It would itemize all of her known expenses and include a review of the aforementioned contracts. But it would also include a "friendship" list: making notes of any deficiencies here and where she would like to develop better rapport.

Her first instinct was to choose her birthday. This is generally not a good idea! There are usually too many distractions around this date. Likewise we avoided the end of year festivity period and yes, her company's year end. It didn't take long to choose a date in mid-May when, as it happened in her case, the Sun passed the position of the Moon in her natal chart.

All cases are different. Nor is it necessary to do this from an astrological stand-point.

The point here is to acknowledge the need for essential financial engine maintenance and to do it!

A Curious Group

On July 24, 1957, had you been standing on the Sun, Pluto appeared to have crossed from the Leo into the Virgo sector of the zodiac. This solar or helio perspective is used by many financial astrologers. From this standpoint, no planet is ever retrograde and the rhythm of each planet's orbit easily seen. Horoscopes though are rarely drawn from this perspective. Most astrologers prefer instead to use of an earth-centered, or geocentric perspective. As a result, the planets (never the Sun or Moon) have periods when they seem to be traveling in reverse: a status termed "retrograde."

From the earth-centered (geocentric) perspective, Pluto appeared to cross into Virgo a little earlier: on October 20, 1956. However, on January 15, 1957, Pluto appeared to slip back into Leo (i.e., became retrograde) before making its final crossing into Virgo on August 19, 1957.

We therefore have a small, but curious group whose horoscopes show Pluto in Leo—but, who, while in the womb, would have experienced the vibration of Pluto in Virgo. I suspect that theirs is a fascinating financial group! My database brings just two examples of people or events born during this period: an insufficient number from which to form judgement. One important event chart from this period is that of the Treaty of Rome, which became the European Economic Union, signed on March 25, 1957.

Clearly the idea for the European Union had been incubating as Pluto made its way through Leo. We can assume that it took on urgency as Pluto made Virgo passage for those few months between October 1956 and January 1957. It was surely felt that this "economic" union was essential (a Virgo word) and would provide an efficient, commercial forum (again, all Virgo keywords).

Yet this union has not been without difficulty and that, I think, is shown by the fact that its Pluto is actually in Leo, not Virgo. Had the Treaty been signed later in the year, with a very definite Pluto in Virgo, it might have quietly gone about its business without quite so many and various crises.

GROUP TWO:
The Pluto in Virgo Generation: 1956–1973

Financial turbulence is to be expected as Pluto moves from one sign to the next. The year 1956 began with a short global recession coinciding with Pluto's move from Leo into Virgo: one of the Earth and Mutable signs of the zodiac. If the Pluto in Leo engine conjures images of one built by Ferrari (speed and glitz), then an engine fashioned in the Virgo style is more BMW or Volvo, i.e., there is greater focus on solidity and efficiency. If this engine has speed capability too, that's a bonus. The accent though is on reliability, space, and capacity. Whereas Pluto in Leo isn't necessarily concerned about the number of people that can be ferried around, or how many items can be squeezed in, Pluto in Virgo most definitely is. It wants and needs to be useful.

The period of 1956–1973 was a complicated one in world history, when many previously held conservative ideals were turned on their head. We can reflect back now on the Flower power of the mid-60s, the Cultural Revolution in China, the students riots in Paris, and much more: agreeing that there was a profound social shift during these years. Pluto's move through Virgo may have been just part of this story; the position of other planets also contributed to the fast-paced developments of this period. We are focused here though on Pluto's position and the influence its position has on financial affairs. Where money matters are concerned, Pluto's Virgo sojourn marked exciting but potentially dangerous developments. It was during this period that the bank guarantee card was introduced, to be followed by the credit card, and shortly after, by the first cash or ATM, machines.

Note the development of systems offering *easy* transfer of funds. Virgo is all about finding efficient ways of working. In 1959, the first machines capable of reading checks were manufactured. It wasn't long before banks were investing heavily in the technology that would eventually deliver automatic teller machines (ATMs) and then, at the end of this period, found yet more ways to further improve the international transfer of funds.

The parents of those born between 1956 and 1973 were

forced to adjust to a very different banking system to that with which they had grown up. Passbooks began to be phased out. No longer did they need to "know" their manager. Indeed, they could go for months without meeting with anyone in charge of their account: the onus was put on individuals to take control of their resources (savings and debt). Individuals were offered a credit limit with their first credit card and, if managed well, later came to rely on that system for their regular financial management.

The personal responsibility of maintaining regularity of payments with a "faceless institution" is very much linked to Pluto's position in Virgo. Before this time, even rent had been collected—often in person by the landlord. With the advent of credit cards and automated banking however, those growing up through these years needed to respond to monthly bills arriving by mail. The debtor did not need to meet the demand immediately but within an agreed period. Some users quickly learned the advantage of buying now and paying later—on occasion without incurring interest or late payment charges. This was very different to a rent collector appearing at the door and waiting for cash to be counted.

As a child—and therefore not in control of the family purse strings—those reaching adulthood during Pluto's transit of Virgo, while not necessarily understanding the financial world around them, may have been aware of elders talking about new ways of handling financial transactions. They may well have witnessed a growing financial confidence in their parents, yet also been aware of a degree of resistance shown by grandparents—bemused and anxious about the growing rise of payment over time-purchase and credit agreements. These children may have overheard heated arguments about the weight of debt and the importance of practicing sound financial management so as not to fall foul of lenders.

Many of those born with Pluto in Virgo witnessed the stress that their parents experienced when they did indeed take on more debt or payments over purchase than they could sustain. Unlike many of their slightly older "Pluto in Leo" friends, some of those born with Pluto in Virgo became involved in household budgeting at a young age: at times even wrestling control from parents who found budgeting hard. This perhaps adds to the Pluto in Virgo generalized financial ability to have various "pots" of money, each designated for specific liabilities. Indeed it is not at all uncommon to discover that these individuals, as they approach and reach retirement, have multiple bank accounts and pension pots.

As an aside, I have been amused by the reaction of those advisors or managers from other generations who are dealing with the estates of those born with Pluto in Virgo. They are often discovering in the process that there is always yet another insurance policy, credit union, or other small account that's been dormant for years but still contains a tidy sum.

Exceptions to the Rule

In the main, those born with Pluto in Virgo practice good financial management, knowing exactly when to service their financial engines and how best to maintain them in optimal condition. They understand the importance of regulation and of budget. Yet there is a subgroup born in the mid 60s who operate entirely differently. This group were born as Uranus moved to conjoin Pluto. Their Plutos operate quite differently: at times rebelling against the idea of working within any kind of constraint whatsoever.

Baulking at the idea of having to conform to what they perceive to be regimented or regular payment system, some have run up huge debts, been ruined, restructured, but then repeated their earlier behavior. In effect, they allow their financial engines to seize through lack of regular maintenance. This sub group were no doubt a trial to their parents many of whom have bailed them out (sometimes more than once).

And yet: in my recent work with clients born essentially between late 1964 and 1966, I have found their response to the idea of practicing financial engineering to be changing—perhaps as a result of bitter experience. As a rule, they are technologically inclined. Though I doubt their ability to keep to a monthly maintenance schedule, I have observed that when given the idea of warning facts and figures (and these vary from person to person), their body language shows them to be interested. I note that two clients born during these years are either married to or have accountants in the family. These connections have proved themselves helpful auditors and regulators.

Another client informed me of a creative system that he had developed: this revolved around agreeing to set a money safety-net level. The person chose—arbitrarily—to use a figure that resonated with his actual birthday. Whether he thought this was a "lucky" figure or not, the fact remained that he then built savings to this level and kept them there. After that he focused on increments—again based on this figure—which seemed to be his personal system of building blocks: an unusual Pluto in Virgo approach to be sure, but one that was clearly working—at least for this person.

Pluto in Virgo Service Record

There is another separation here, dividing this group into two types: the larger Pluto in Virgo population, and those born during that curious period in the 1960s as Uranus was within a few degrees of Pluto, and both were opposed to Saturn and Chiron. (Chiron is the planetoid that orbits between Saturn and Uranus. It is generally prominent in the charts of those with a life focus of healing, problem-solving, and of taking unusual approaches to fixing that which is "wrong.") The birth charts of those born between 1964 and 1967 contain this curious and special planetary picture. To deal with this unusual group first:

It is not unusual for engines to be returned to dealer workshops for regular maintenance. In this way, the dealer and the owner can keep a regular check on conditions and help guarantee positive results. Financial affairs should be treated in the same way: with regular maintenance.

Yet some of those born between 1964 and 1968 have shown greater inclination to wait until breakdown before taking action—at times "fixing things" themselves, and so deferring the need for advice. That "system," however, has often led these individuals to require urgent accounting advice so as not to fall foul of debt collectors or tax inspectors. Sadly, they have not always chosen mentors wisely—often paying considerable sums before discovering that they could have found better service for less. Many now have a tainted financial record compromising their ability to gain credit even today. Repairing a poor credit record is never easy.

With the exception of this curious age-group, Pluto in Virgo people are more inclined to maintain a good credit record. Though some do not use credit at all. This group has shown a preference to behave as earlier generations—with a "save first, spend later" policy. Clearly if they have gone down the route of "no credit," then there is always the potential for difficulty when they are older: most probably when Pluto arrives in the sign opposite to Virgo, Pisces, in 2040.

With the exception of these two subsets, those with Pluto in Virgo, in the main have unblemished financial service records and should be regarded as well placed to cope with the tumultuous financial seas ahead.

Even the "mid 60s" group have an ability to keep their ears to the ground and are often in tune with developments in technical or health-related industries. They might even be serial entrepreneurs. Though the financial record-keeping of this particular group may leave much to be desired, experience has taught them the value of having loyal book-keepers and accountants (actually, more usually partners) on the payroll.

Even then, I have seen difficulties. My experience of this mid-60s group is that their business planning is unusual to say the least. When facing business collapse, they claim that they lacked funding, that banks were unsympathetic, or that their ideas were ahead of their time, and so their businesses failed. It is as likely that they grossly underestimated the discipline and qualifications required for success.

* * *

Those born when Uranus was NOT conjoined with Pluto (broadly before 1964 or after 1968—though a professional and experienced astrologer would look very closely for planetary connections) have the kind of financial service records to be expected where Virgo is involved: awareness of the value of good record keeping. They know that regular assessment of their financial systems is wise and are willing to make change as needed. Though they may not be serial entrepreneurs, they are often serial investors: moving savings so as to achieve optimum deals.

With regard to investment, they take keen interest (sometimes too keen in that they monitor price changes so regularly they worry about fluctuations that tend to smooth out if monitored less frequently). They know too that there is merit in spreading risk through property, commodities, and equities.

Perhaps because Virgo is one of the Mutable (adaptable) signs of the zodiac, those born with Pluto in this position seem to have an inherent understanding of shifting trends and an innate (at times uncanny) ability to be ahead of the pack. Consider those who saw the value of media, data management, or genetic-engineering stocks before others were anywhere near acknowledging, let alone investing in these stocks. Not only did these people make excellent profit, as they learned more about the potential of these growing and now deemed essential (internet and mobile phone companies), they also moved to seize other opportunities.

Here in London we had a small astrological share group in the late 1990s. The age group was quite narrow; encompassing those with Pluto in either Leo or Virgo. The former group were there mostly for the fun and social side, while the Pluto in Virgo group wanted to see their money put to work. It was the latter group who made greatest contribution by focusing on company charts. (It is a long story, but readers might like to know that the group was disbanded ahead of the Dot Com crisis in May 2000 at no loss to the shareholders. While there was not much financial gain either long-term friendships were made and kept).

The key fact to remember with those with Pluto in Virgo is that they make it a priority for their money to work for them. Though this is of course a generalization, they work hard—as hard as their financial advisors—to ensure that money matters are given respect and attention.

It is normal for the service record of those with Pluto in Virgo to be good and above average, though that does not mean that they have not gone through lean times. However, even if they experienced default or other financial difficulty, they can usually show that they tackled the problems and moved on.

This type of success rate is particularly true of that period between 1996 and 2008, when Pluto passed through the next of the Mutable signs, Sagittarius. By then, the considerable world and financial experience of the Pluto in Virgo group was likely enough for them to award themselves masters degrees in administration. If any group was well placed to ride the global financial crisis and its legacies, it was surely those with Pluto in Virgo. With their "fingers in many pies," and their attention to detail, they were able to take fast and prompt action as problems surfaced. While they may well have experienced a wild financial ride through this period, that experience is likely to stand them in good stead should they live long enough to experience Pluto's journey through the next of the Mutable signs—Pisces, from 2038 through 2043.

Before 2043, and as Pluto makes its way through Aquarius, it is probable that those with Pluto in Virgo will focus on investing in essential services. Drawn to community projects and to any kind of investment (property included) where they see their cash at work, and noting other people's developing motivations and desires, they may choose to invest in services that at the time of writing are not yet available but which will eventually be much in demand. Of these, "digital death management and inner city farming projects" are likely to appeal.

Pluto in Virgo Engine Maintenance

With the exception of those born in the mid 60s, whose cavalier approach often results in their financial problems, the majority of those with Pluto positioned in Virgo keep their financial engines in good working order. They often have a fascination with developments in fashion and business and keep up to date with trends. If they hold shares, they check the movement of prices often. The financial advisor who maintains annual contact, and who is available during the year for queries, will be much appreciated. They like knowing details: indeed, a "quick look" or "broad brush-stroke" approach does not work for them. They are at home with spread sheets, projections, and generally enjoy the challenge of risk assessment before taking action.

Many of these people made their first investments as Pluto moved into the Water sign of Scorpio (1983–1995) and some did quite well. Other saw the vulnerability of certain companies and the potential for them to be taken over by larger conglomerates. They bought in and realized profit at the subsequent take-over when their assessments proved correct. Some brought properties that they later flipped at a profit.

With confidence boosted by gains made between 1984 and 1989, they negotiated the travails of the low in the business cycle (1989–1990) and were at the head of the queue as new opportunities became available in the early 1990s.

Indeed, by the time Pluto had moved into Sagittarius (the next Mutable sign) in 1995, they had identified areas ripe for further expansion (usually emerging markets). Nor were they surprised when the global financial system came to near breakdown as Pluto moved from Sagittarius to Capricorn (2008). Their natural instincts and diligence in monitoring the health of banks and companies resulted in many having moved away from blue chip stocks ahead of the calamity. They were then well-placed to buy back in at market lows and have reaped considerable profit since as share prices have risen.

But what next?

Even ahead of the probable turbulent times likely to be experienced as Pluto moves from Capricorn to Aquarius in 2023, banking systems will probably be restructured. Indeed, it is felt by some that 2020 will be the year of the great financial reset.

To keep the Pluto in Virgo engine in good condition through the coming years, it is arguably important that this group focus on items and services deemed essential to sustain life. Some of these investments might seem boring, but, assuming that the companies involved have sound financial structures, they should at the very least yield solid reliable dividends.

The "awkward set" born with in the mid 60s might not be inspired by this approach even if it does offer a safety net. Their preference may be for data management companies. Perhaps they will find these more exciting—though the caveat here is that these firms still need to have a robust financial base and sound operating controls if they are to realize profit.

All of those with Pluto in Virgo should have the edge when it comes to identifying trends. Though much may be made of the need to "get back to basics," those from the mid 60s will surely be aware of technical developments and the new products and related services that move quickly from "nice ideas" to "essential item" status. The products and services associated with such developments will surely take off from 2023 after Pluto moves into Aquarius. It is not hard to imagine the mid 60s group realizing profit, even as others find that the reliable dividends trail off in 2025.

GROUP THREE
The Pluto in Libra Generation: 1973–1984

From 1973 to 1984, Pluto passed through Libra: spending a shorter time passing through this sign than through others, owing to the elliptical nature of its orbit. As was the case as Pluto moved from Leo to Virgo, this crossing-over period also began with a recession. Rather than lasting just two quarters of a single year, as had been the case previously, this recession lasted a couple of years. Some will remember the increased oil price of 1973 and 1974. UK readers might remember the power cuts that led to a three-day work week. Though this activity can be traced back to the oil crisis of that time, many developments indicated a profound economic shift.

The global upheaval that we might now recognize as part of the transition of Pluto from Virgo to Libra actually began as Pluto was in the last degrees of Virgo. President Nixon was faced with difficult economic data. His decision that the US should leave the Bretton Woods agreement meant that the US dollar was no longer to be backed by physical gold. By 1973, the dollar was floating against other currencies—as it does to this day.

Pluto in the Air-sign Libra is very different than Pluto in Earth-sign Virgo. Pluto in Libra thrives on ideas and fluctuating values. Note that Libra is the sign of the scales: balance is all important. So too is comparison. It was during this period, and with air travel becoming affordable for many, that a growing number of people learned about currency exchange and varying rates. This proved a steep learning curve for a lot of people.

The International SWIFT banking system was developed in 1973. It was the first of many developments in the field of global banking that has led to the world becoming a "global village."

Those born during these years are now in their 40s and 50s. They have adapted to a world of financial "ideas." Whereas their forebears carried coins and notes, these people have wallets full of credit cards whose worth is often unquantifiable. They carry both debit and credit cards and juggle between the two. Many have mortgages offset against savings. Their financial engines might even be described as "twin engine or more" as they move funds from one place to another.

Their financial world is so very different than that of their grandparents, many of whom are still mystified by contact-less cards and internet banking. Yet even this generation with Pluto in Libra may soon be challenged by the changing financial rhythms of the coming decade.

There is a tendency for those with Pluto in Libra to talk about what they ought to be doing financially but not necessarily taking action. They have plans but not necessarily the energy or competence to carry these through. (As throughout this work we are making generalizations—only a review of the individual chart will determine if this is likely to be the case).

If you are at all familiar with the keywords associated with the zodiac signs, then you won't be surprised by the desire for improved financial efficiency that marks the difference between the Pluto in Leo and Pluto in Virgo generations. Those with Pluto in Libra, and born between 1973 and 1984, are different yet again. Their preference is for a gently purring financial engine requiring little maintenance, yet capable of moving to warp speed when required—again demanding as little preparatory effort as necessary! Attaining this goal has proved a struggle, and may well turn out to be a life-long quest.

Pluto's arrival in this sign in 1972 marked the beginning of a recession that was followed by a period of inflation. Buoyed by promising employment and rosy financial figures, United States President Nixon was elected in 1972. It soon became apparent that all was not running as smoothly as had been thought. Though many put the blame on rising oil prices, it is now generally agreed that the monetary policy decisions taken during his time in office exacerbated difficulties. Few companies came to market during this period: there were some months when no IPO was offered. Existing businesses struggled and many were declared bankrupt. This "chief financial officer" of the USA was a man with no formal training in economics. Indeed, he himself was eventually declared bankrupt. This was not a period when financial engines purred.

The generation with Pluto in Libra grew up against the backdrop of commercial challenge and of rising interest rates. They witnessed financial struggles as their parents coped with a now unthinkable rise in interest rates rising above sixteen percent under Nixon's successor Jimmy Carter. No doubt many of these children were privy to arguments driven by financial concerns. Families split up under the pressures of this period.

A clear legacy of these childhoods is the determination to "do whatever" to avoid being left vulnerable. At an often unconscious level those of this group go to great lengths to feel financially secure though some have eschewed material wealth altogether. (There is a known subset from this age group who have actively chosen very simple life-styles away from materialism, and even a few for whom homelessness is a chosen way of life).

Libra is one of the Air signs, and as you might imagine, generally gives careful thought to husbanding resources. Pluto though is a very slow moving planet. It is helpful then to think of heavy Air whose weight at times can be crushing and suffocating. It's often said that those born under Sun-sign Libra avoid decision-making. This is a little harsh. True, Libras often don't relish the effort of weighing things up carefully. Where financial matters are concerned they can easily feel bombarded by information and paralysed by the sheer quantity to be considered.

For this reason they tend to be slow to judgment and, once made, prefer to adopt a system or portfolio intended to last. The process of engine overhaul is, to them, messy and tricky: not something to be done if it can be avoided. Indeed, it may be true to say that having taken the decision of where to invest, they are so exhausted by the process, that they can barely contemplate reviewing their portfolio.

Relationships—and especially equally balanced financial partnerships—often feature in discussions with clients born during between 1973 and 1984. You may recall that it was during this period when "going dutch" became a feature of dating and courtship.

In 1986, one of the first business charts I was called on to interpret was of a catering company, launched a decade earlier by two mothers. Until 1984, they had an equal share in the business both in terms of time and money. All had gone well until—almost to the day—when Pluto moved into Scorpio, and rifts appeared. Each was feeling the other was taking more from the business than was her due. (The business limped along until 1990 and finally closed). The point to make here is that businesses formed during Pluto's transit of Libra demand equitable splits at every level.

Those with Pluto in Libra expect equal partnership: demanding that those entrusted with their savings treat that cash as if it were their own. They have a preference for the "personal touch" and value financial advisors who take the time to get to know them. They do not do well with faceless companies, and do best when they have a personal manager or agent whom they can call and who is familiar with their position.

One of the very interesting features of those with this placement concerns their attitude to property investment. Here they appear divided into two groups: those who managed to get on to the ladder and those who are still struggling to do so. Many of the latter may never manage to do so—prices having ridden so high, and now quite out of reach without significant assistance from "the bank of Mom and Dad."

As might be expected whenever the sign of the scales is involved, balance can easily be disturbed. Whereas those with Pluto in Virgo require explanations as to why profits haven't been as expected, those with Pluto in Libra accept that not everything can be perfect. Rather than hold regular post-mortems, they are more inclined to take advice, cut losses, and move on to new pastures.

As explained, as any one of the slow moving planets changes signs, the event often coincides with marked financial developments. These developments present fresh challenge to all generations. Some, however, will negotiate these with more ease than others.

Those with Pluto in Libra will be faced with three very different and contrasting challenges between 2023 and 2026. They will need to cope with imbalance before their financial engines are rebalanced.

It is reasonable to suppose that they might even enjoy surfing the waves following Pluto's arrival in Air sign Aquarius in 2023. It is not unknown for this group to keep a keen "ear to the ground," and in so doing, be alert to developments even ahead of companies reaching their initial public offering stage. It is entirely possible that those able to invest will tune in to new financial currents and get in on the ground floor.

They may find that investments made after Jupiter and Saturn align at the start of Aquarius in late 2020 bring reward in 2023, when probable fast progress attracts takeover interest. Though the charts for each of these companies (and of the investor) would need to be considered, small investments made—probably in social media and technical companies—will lead to a rapid rise in the share value of these initially small enterprises. It is, of course, to be expected that those born with Pluto in Libra be keen investors in these: either at designer, entrepreneurial, or investor level.

While Pluto's move into the Air-sign Aquarius should provide a boost to this generation, this ingress is followed by Neptune's arrival into Libra's opposite sign, Aries in 2025. To date, Neptune's transit of a Fire sign (Aries, Leo, or Sagittarius) has coincided with rising interest rates and, at times (especially when Jupiter joins

Neptune in a Fire sign as will be the case between July 2026 and July 2027), with rampant inflation. Gains made could so easily be lost.

If we add to this, Uranus' move into another of the Air signs, Gemini, we have a different challenge. We can reasonably conclude that, although there will likely be great demand for the communication systems coming to market in 2026, some of those launched between 2021 and 2023 will be rendered redundant. Indeed, some of the companies showing so much promise early in that decade could be bankrupted when demand fails. It is imperative that the Pluto in Libra generation be aware of the potential for financial disaster through over-investing during that earlier period.

Service History

You could be forgiven for thinking that those with any planet in Libra would avoid mess and dirt. Yet those with Pluto in this sign are well aware that occasionally it's necessary to get one's hands dirty. Changing engine parts is usually a messy experience. Though the Pluto in Libra group may be aware that their engine isn't purring well enough—and mention it to others—they tend to delay action until a part (investment) seizes up. Indeed, they might not even notice that dividends aren't being made for some time. Much as they might wish that they were on top of their investments and long-term financial planning, all too often other matters get in the way. They tend to wait too long before taking remedial action, such as moving their investment portfolio from one agency to another.

Very often they are driven to action by crisis: change of job, house purchase, or other major event. Though clearly these events affect everyone at some stage in our lives, it seems to be a peculiar facet of those with Pluto in Libra. It may only be when going through a major upheaval that they give full attention to financial matters: probing reports for clues as to why certain areas haven't done as well as expected, and comparing deals new to market since they last signed contracts. They may profess that the idea of an annual review appeals to them and even enjoy that process when it's underway. "Balancing the books" is a phrase well suited to this group! However, and often because they leave it so long between one in-depth review and the next, they find that there is considerable work involved and then require the service of professionals to assist them through what they then see as a financial minefield.

Those with Pluto in Libra are highly sensitive to financial fluctuations. It could be said that they actively try to avoid situations where their funds are subjected to the vagaries of daily market trading. Where possible, they will choose fixed rate deals so that at all times they know where they stand so that their balance should not be disturbed.

Whereas those with Pluto in Virgo are wholly familiar with the exact dimensions of each component, those with Pluto in Libra worry less about this (or indeed the quality of the parts used), but are on high alert for any deviation in the fine-tuning and the sounds their financial engine makes. It is especially important they use this gift wisely between 2023 and 2025 and move away from investments where technology is changing so fast that the product or service becomes redundant.

Maintaining the Engine

Tax matters—obviously. To those with Pluto in Libra it really, really matters. This group were hit hard by the global financial crash when it became clear that systems in which they were supposed to trust were not up to the job. They learned that you can't leave long-term financial planning to experts. And now they know that they need to be cautious about placing confidence in governments and regulated systems. They understand that rules around inheritance and pensions will inevitably change before they reach their later lives. Perhaps more than any previous generation they know that at some point they will have to assume control.

Yet having that knowledge and acting upon it though are two different things. They are well aware of the need to have information ready for end of tax year, and know that they ought also to set aside time to assess their general financial position. Yet they can—and usually do—find some way to engage in a displacement activity rather than face the task.

That said, in recent years I have been impressed by those of this group who have made wills and who have kept these up to date. This essential exercise is not a million miles from financial audit. Their thinking process demands that they give careful thought to general inheritance issues. Property often requires particular attention—with many seeing property as their best pension.

Another common feature has been investment either in their own hobbies (which may yet provide another revenue stream in time), and in the Arts. Indeed, the latter may prove to be one of their key investment areas. Generally they require little encouragement to learn more about the advantages of this type of investment.

One engine maintenance task that this group seem to enjoy hugely is attending auctions or buying and selling on Ebay. Though those born a little later with Pluto in Scorpio do better still, the talents of those with Pluto in Libra to buy and sell in this way is not be ignored.

Since late 2010, Uranus has been moving through Libra's opposite sign, Aries. Since then many of those with Pluto in Libra have been thinking "out of the box." I suspect that they have already made shrewd investments without knowing. Once Pluto arrives in Aquarius (the next of the Air signs), those moves may well provide dividends.

Their more immediate investment and maintenance move is likely to revolve around insurance. Between 2018 and 2023, they may find this market attractive. Some could reap benefits from re-insurance schemes, where insurers themselves are insured.

Another promising investment area will surely be security. They may be drawn to companies providing services or products in this fast-growing sector. While generally resistant to too complicated a portfolio, they are often attracted to specific areas.

GROUP FOUR:
The Pluto in Scorpio Generation: 1983–1995

I wonder if you have read Michael Lewis' *Liar's Poker*—a wonderful tale of the "Greed is Good" philosophy that dominated from the mid to late 80s, or, in astrological terms, as Pluto transited Scorpio. This was the Yuppie period, a time of "big business and mega-takeover." Many found it an exhilarating time; as many others found it dispiriting, and the practices of those big businesses simply ruthless. A number of the now large global corporations made successful take-over bids during this period allowing them to become apparently unassailable empires. Pluto is viewed as the "God of the Underworld," a powerful force that can dethrone or empower at will. Its influence is compelling: a major force that is both magnetic and forceful as we saw when its arrival in Capricorn coincided with pressure on the banking system.

Those businesses which grew super-large between 1983 and 1995 could find their existence threatened as Pluto moves through Aquarius between 2023 and 2036.

Now let's consider the Pluto in Scorpio profile. It is built around power and designed to work at full throttle, to cut through ice or to battle great waves as necessary. This engine is exquisite to look at; shiny, efficient, large, and, when working, throbbing with a thrilling pulse. Every component is made by the best and using the best. It is also designed to last, to work as well in fifty years as it does on its first day. This is the engine that goes "round the clock" several times over.

Its weakness? This engine requires expert piloting: engineers and captains par excellence. In the hands of a novice, this engine can be broken. It requires the care of at least a partnership, if not a team, to keep this engine well-oiled and in condition. At least one member of this team needs to be monitoring every sound and movement, and to cope with the intense heat it generates. Given its mesmerizing power, it's often the case that this engine receives visitors: people who want to see it at work and wish to emulate its performance. Unless they too have Pluto in Scorpio, it's unlikely that this is achievable.

Those with Pluto in Scorpio work as much on instinct as they do on knowledge. They can't always explain their financial acumen—often professing bewilderment that anyone thinks that what they have is different or special.

Though of course it's not true in every case, a significant number of clients with Pluto in Scorpio have been faced with issues around legacies and inheritance, or have been asked by others to assist in their financial dealings. In time I suspect that they will make first class executors.

The Pluto in Scorpio engine runs on the equivalent of fossil fuels. In investment terms, these individuals are draw to companies that have stood the test of time and yes, may be energy providers.

Just as companies in the 80s made their takeover bids, buying out those unable to fend off approaches, so it seems that individuals born with Scorpio have a flair for seeing what can be turned around and used again. They have a happy knack for revitalizing that which is apparently wasted or unwanted. These are the people who find "cash in the attic"—often, that attic belonging to someone else!

Pluto made its first Scorpio ingress on November 5, 1983— moving back into Libra for a few months in 1984—before making full ingress on August 28, 1984. Pluto did not move on into Sagittarius until November 1995.

Scorpio is associated with the world of high finance. It should come as no surprise that as Pluto made Scorpio ingress, there was a major development in the world of banking. In 1983, customers of the Nottingham Building Society in the United Kingdom were offered the first ever Internet banking service by the Bank of Scotland. This "Homelink" service offered those with a television set and telephone line, the ability to send transfers and pay bills. By the close of Pluto's Scorpio ingress, such services were incorporated into Microsoft's technology via Money Manager software. These developments changed the way in which many customers use banking services forever.

As we now know to be a common feature of Pluto's move from one sign to another, there was also a financial crisis. Black

Saturday describes the low point for the Hong Kong dollar with one US dollar buying 9.6 Hong Kong dollars (HKD). At the start of 1983, that same US dollar bought just 6.5 HKD. This signalled a huge wave of currency dealing and led to major developments in foreign exchange trading.

Yet another feature of Pluto's Scorpio period was an extraordinary number of hostile takeovers. The size of global corporations swelled as the world became an ever-smaller trading village. Perhaps though, the most important feature of this period was deregulation of the London Stock Market: an action now known as "Big Bang": the result of an agreement reached in 1983 as Pluto made Scorpio ingress, and which changed trading rules at the London Stock Exchange. This had a singular impact across the world when the rules were implemented on October 26, 1986. Big Bang led to the takeover of many old firms by younger banks and the dawn of a new financial age.

By the time Pluto left Scorpio, the landscape of the world of finance was alien to many. New instruments (now termed weapons of mass financial destruction) were developed with even the most seasoned of financiers at a loss to explain their complexity.

Though the parents of those born between 1983 and 1995 as Pluto moved through Scorpio were no doubt oblivious to these developments, many were lured into thinking that their savings and investments could only increase in value. As they were to learn, the extraordinary vehicles through which their mortgages were serviced, were later unable to deliver promised returns. Only those who were risk averse and financially astute came through this period without experiencing significant financial wounding.

The children born as Pluto moved through Scorpio became aware that they should not "put all eggs in one basket" and that their investments should be as diverse as possible. They learned through the financial debacles experienced by their elders that debt is onerous and that there is no such thing as a guaranteed return on savings.

Scorpio Service Record

So far the Pluto in Scorpio generation have shown natural ability to financially recharge. Clients with this placement have displayed an at times uncanny gift for both investment and saving. This was the group who came of age at the Millennium. While two clients were caught up in the Dot-com debacle of that year, to be clear, they didn't lose; but their parents did. Both have chosen to help their parents cope with those losses. Their parents in effect gave them a master class in the importance of undertaking careful risk assessment—an area in which I have since seen evidence of excellence. In the case of one client (a Taurus with Pluto in Scorpio) who chose not to go on into higher education for fear of incurring a burden of debt, she instead chose to self-invest and established a neat business focused on recycling.

It will surely come as no surprise to those familiar with the traits associated with each sign that those born with Pluto in Scorpio have natural detective skills. They ask good questions and will always test the bottom line.

Another client from this group eventually bought out the family business: most likely not at full price. But even so, my understanding is that she took some time before making the decision to make this purchase and carried out many checks before going ahead. Apparently there had been a time in the late 1980s (while still at school), when she was aware that the business might need to go into receivership. Though she had little understanding as to what this might really mean, it seems she tuned into the idea of being left with nothing, and her latent risk-averseness was switched on! It is this that has since propelled her on to achieve great things but, so far, to resist the temptation to expand her niche business. She continues to contain and enjoy her success.

Two other clients from this group experienced parental loss before their 24th birthdays. Their respective fathers had each been attempting to avoid bankruptcy. These young clients were left with the unpleasant task of negotiating with creditors, even while grief-stricken. Both have since shown a remarkable gift for saving and investing, though neither seems to have had to forfeit much enjoyment in the process. They can operate "on a shoe string." Their earlier experience has also given them confidence to tackle administrative matters and to negotiate and improve offered financial terms.

The service records of those with Pluto in Scorpio—though I have not seen thousands of charts from this group—shown an innate ability to conserve, repair and rebuild where necessary. In the aftermath of the global financial crisis I have seen evidence of their ability to apply austerity measures, review their situation, consolidate, and now, as they emerge from that dark tunnel, give thought as to how best to move on and invest.

Maintenance

Maintaining the Pluto in Scorpio financial engine requires constant awareness of the pulse of that engine. Those with Pluto in this sign generally feel difficulties before others do. They have no need to wait for their annual health check but are highly tuned to even the briefest of disruptions in smooth running and are alert to when adjustments must be made.

They seem to know when to adjust their sails, divest of an investment that fails to deliver reward, and to move on. Though it is also true that those with Pluto in Scorpio—and with the Sun in one of the Fixed signs of Taurus, Leo, Scorpio or Aquarius—hold on to the last minute in the hope that a trend will change. It is not the case that those with Fixed sign emphasis are wholly resistant to adopting new tactics, but more the case that they double-check to see if anything can be salvaged before moving on.

If we accept that the financial waters might become more like rapids between 2023 and 2026, then it is surely imperative for everyone to ensure that they have life jackets at the ready ahead of Pluto's Aquarius ingress.

Perhaps no group will be quite as well prepared to navigate the torrid waters ahead as those born between 1984 and 1995. They are naturally disposed to thinking that catastrophe is never far away and know that having lifeboats in good order is essential. Even so, they may be dismayed to discover that the foundations of those business establishments which they assumed to be "safe" are anything but. Included in this "safe" group may be mutual societies and life-insurance companies. Yet these businesses, in particular, will surely find Pluto's transit of Aquarius particularly challenging and may be unable to pay expected dividends. To guard against losses here, an alternative for those with Pluto in Scorpio may be to consider investments in precious jewels or works of art: tangible assets that can be sold as necessary.

Whereas those with Pluto in Scorpio have generally been aware that by buying quality (albeit a sometimes recycled but known brand) they receive the most reliability, Neptune's Aries ingress will doubtless bring the realization that they have to make changes. Taking into account Uranus's coincident move into Gemini, they may find that their financial goals can only be realized by adapting their engines to use new fuels. For example, they may no longer be able to rely on dividends from older companies, but must be agile and technically proficient. This may involve learning to move money or master block-chain technology to stay afloat.

GROUP FIVE:
The Pluto in Sagittarius Generation: 1995–2008

While the majority of those with Pluto in Sagittarius are still too young to have any appreciable financial record, it is possible to make some assumptions. Sagittarius is both a Fire and Muta-ble sign. Put the two factors together and it's not hard to con-jure up an image of multiple fires, or imagine these individuals as being pre-primed to have their investment fingers in multiple pies. Those born with Pluto in this area of the zodiac will likely use several engines to run their financial affairs: with each of those engines using different types of fuel.

We must remember that even those of this group born in the very early years of Pluto's Sagittarius journey would not have been in charge of their financial affairs during the global financial crisis of 2007–2008. The majority would still be at school. Yet that does not mean that they were unaffected by those events or unaware of their impact.

With news bulletins dominated by the crisis, many, even at a very young age, were asking adults what it all meant. Even the five and six-year-olds would have been aware that banks—even if they did not understand what these institutions did or were supposed to do—were collapsing. It's perhaps true to say that all of those with Pluto in Sagittarius were—unlike any other generation— alerted to the fact that these "mysterious organizations" were not necessarily stable.

They were presumably also made aware of the shock and distress felt by many who lost their jobs overnight. Instinctively they would have learned the importance of having savings or other financial safety nets. For the very many whose parents or grandparents did not have a financial cushion, witnessing the distress of these adults must have been painful. Those old enough even to understand a little of the crisis surely absorbed the painful lesson that putting all savings eggs in one basket had been a disastrous move for many adults, and that those who did ride the financial storm benefited from spreading those savings across a variety of funds.

Perhaps it is then unsurprising that those with Pluto in Sagittarius are choosing to develop multiple nest eggs. This is the generation willing to switch suppliers annually, and who put effort into finding the best possible deals. Though the sign of Sagittarius is often noted for a certain careless or cavalier approach to finance, that does not appear to be the case for the majority of those born with Pluto in that sign. Rather, they are showing prudence— presumably developed as a result of witnessing the chaos that followed the global financial crisis.

The youngest of this generation are only now entering their teen years. Many will be aware of the ongoing discussion about how expensive homes are and the difficulty that young people will have in getting onto the housing ladder. Already, for many, this achievement will not—and may never be—one of their financial aims. Arguably, one of the only ways in which they might be able to achieve house-owning status will be through joining forces with friends in similar positions. Between 2025 and 2033, we may well see an extraordinary rise in the number of friends who choose to cohabit and co-share the financial responsibility of their nests.

Again, whereas other generations tended, if they did invest, to focus on local stock exchanges, those born between 1995 and 2008 as Pluto moved through Sagittarius appear willing to venture further afield: considering emerging markets with as much interest as local ones. If you are at all familiar with the traits associated with the sign of Sagittarius you will perhaps not be surprised to note that those with Pluto in this sign often put ethical concerns at the heart of their portfolios. Though I have as yet only seen a few clients from this age group, in each case they have told me about investments that they view as being both financially prudent for their savings plans but also philanthropic. On two occasions I have been surprised to be asked whether the chart favored certain parts of the world. In both those occasions the individuals had invested in small companies. Neither country would be classed as an official emerging market at the time of writing, but no doubt will be in the coming decade.

Bearing in mind the still-youthfulness of this generation, it is understandable that many have yet to develop their investment strategies. Yet instinctively they are likely aware that they want to have a variety of plans—at least at their disposal if not to participate in as yet. Financial advisors then should be aware that this group will likely ask many, many questions and about areas of investment in which those advisors may have little knowledge. It could be that the Pluto in Sagittarius group choose to be their own advisors, sharing information and advising one another.

In keeping with their age, this Pluto in Sagittarius group is still self investing. They are as they say, still "finding their way in the world." Realizing that the way forward isn't necessarily with the University degree that earlier generations felt imperative, it seems they're putting every effort into ensuring that they have a rounded CV illustrating multiple experience and interest in many areas.

Maintenance

Maintaining the Pluto in Sagittarius financial engine is probably best done by keeping abreast both of innovation and of world developments. Many are natural explorers and know that to keep their various physical, financial, and spiritual motors in good order, they need to be in a position to spread their wings: if not through travel, then certainly through engaging with those involved in global enterprises.

While many of the older generations have fears about developments in artificial intelligence rendering their occupations redundant, those with Pluto in Sagittarius may well be investing in AI companies. Their financial engines will undoubtedly include interest in the development of information technology: most obviously through social media.

In terms of maintenance, this group values a daily information feed. It is unlikely that an annual meeting with a financial advisor will suit them: rather they might prefer monthly meetings— perhaps even taking part in an active investment group. Initially they might drink or party away their profits. But from 2021, and with Jupiter and Saturn in Aquarius, they may be rather more inclined to build and protect their nest eggs.

GROUP SIX:
The Pluto in Capricorn Generation: 2008–2023

Even the oldest of those born with Pluto in Capricorn are only in their pre-high school years at the time of writing and there is no service record for us to consider. However, I think we can make educated guesses as to how these people will use and maintain their financial engines.

First and foremost, we should consider engine size. Capricorn is often depicted as a goat at the top of a mountain: an image not just of climbing to success but of the perspective gained from reaching the top. The Pluto in Capricorn financial motor must be built to last, have considerable power, and be able to cover long, long distances before being reconditioned. Carrying spare parts will also be necessary, as it is probable that resources will be needed for journeys far from mission control (and spare parts!). Unsurprisingly then, we should expect those with Pluto in this sign to have extra savings plans hidden away "just in case."

With Pluto in Capricorn the individual is likely to play for the long term. That does not mean that they won't expose themselves to risk but that that risk, will be based on qualified reporting and approved research.

Those with Pluto in this sign may not be so dissimilar in their approach to savings as their Pluto in Cancer (Capricorn's opposite sign) great-great grandparents born in the early part of the twentieth century. Like their ancestors, they may eschew borrowing wherever possible and instead choose to save first, buy later. They will also be motivated to build financial engines capable of coping with either storm or pirate attack.

We should note that many of this group may well outlive earlier generations by several decades. Covering the costs of their later years may be a fact that they are made aware of early in life—especially if they see other generations (notably those with Pluto in Libra) facing financial difficulty in their twilight years. They will not wish to replicate this.

If this group does indeed reach their centenaries, they will experience Pluto's journey through Aquarius, Pisces, Aries, and Taurus. The toughest part of their financial journeys will most likely come as Pluto moves through Aries (2066–2095) when there may be periods where they feel that their asset base is being compromised and that they are powerless to protect their savings.

Yet though they may well experience a difficult decade, it should be remembered that this generation is likely to have spread risks as Pluto made its way through Pisces. They may well have placed savings in many different areas so that when upheaval is experienced in one sector, it is compensated for by promise elsewhere.

It seems reasonable to suggest that once Pluto reaches Pisces, those with Pluto in Capricorn at birth will benefit from undertaking up-to-the-minute financial training courses accessing the required knowledge to know how best to move investments with ease: effectively putting in place damage limitation should the stormy seas of 2043–2066 threaten their asset base.

Servicing and Maintenance

We can assume that those with Pluto in Capricorn will undertake regular maintenance review. That they will have used the best advisors available, and that their service records will be complete. Though as Pluto moved through Capricorn many people lost respect for financial advisors—whose advice they feel left them vulnerable during the global financial crisis of 2007–2008— by the time Pluto reaches Pisces, the reputation of these advisors should be restored. Those with Pluto in Capricorn may be first in the queue for their services: at the very least for an annual financial health check, but they will likely be carrying out their own monthly wealth checks during the year as well.

Conclusion

With, in order, Pluto (2023), Neptune (March 2025), and Uranus (July 2025) after a minimum of seven years moving into new areas of the zodiac, the financial seas ahead will be choppy. The six types of financial engine identified through Pluto's position, will have to find different ways to sail through these torrents. Some will need extra care and maintenance, whereas those that are younger (e.g., Pluto in Capricorn), may find the first stage of their financial journey exciting, if challenging. Difficulties will surely come up since they have no earlier experience or credit rating to access. This group does not yet know the full capabilities of their vehicles.

Given the probable collapse of bond markets and the high level of world debt yet to be addressed, world governments will have to find new ways to collect taxes to pay for essential services. Before leaving port, our finances may be examined by authorities and charged (extra tax) before we can even go forward. Even the provisions carefully placed on board might not be safe. Property, gold etc., etc. could be confiscated again.

Our engines though remain ours. Familiarizing ourselves with their operation, ensuring that they are given due care and attention to be in optimum working order, is our personal responsibility. Achieving positive results will require assistance from professionals: financial advisors, astrologers, and other mentors.

We should also be aware that the exposure of corruption in many non-government agencies will probably lead to the collapse of these organizations. By the time that Pluto reaches Pisces in 2043, charities too may find that their support base dwindling and that they can no longer supply aid.

Protecting oneself from events quite beyond human control likely means giving careful thought to "safe" areas of the world and assessing the viability of moving to these. This risk-assessment is something to which we should all give careful thought. The likely difficulties brought about through changes in weather patterns will leave many people destitute. This is clearly not our preferred situation. We will all surely seek comfort and security in our later years.

Defining our financial destination, as stated many times here, will depend on our personal charts. With confidence in our respective engines, and understanding of when these will require special care and attention, we can then focus on plotting the course ahead. And let us never forget that aside from meeting our own financial needs, we may be called upon to give assistance to others.

CHAPTER 2

Plotting Your Course and Investment Strategy

Before setting the engines to full speed ahead you should plot your course. While you might adjust your destination en route, it is a good idea to have a clear idea of your aims and objectives before leaving port. Plotting a course to safe port requires care—and should include an understanding of your ability to stay on track and knowledge of the ingrained habits that might sabotage your journey.

Destination

Priority one is, of course, to survive! Solar conditions may be such that even despite mankind's best endeavors, there are changes in terrestrial weather conditions that threaten life in ways beyond our control. Assuming that we are not imperilled by various weather catastrophes, we may consider that as well as having sufficient funds to secure our old age, we might wish to leave a lasting legacy—both within our families and, perhaps, at the philanthropic level. Taking time to consider our legacy is thus another valuable exercise.

Many studies have shown that those who have a clear idea of their destination are most likely to succeed. It is worthwhile noting aims and objectives—even if they presently seem fanciful. These should include, from the financial perspective, the age at which you wish to retire and the area of the world in which you'd like to pass your remaining years. With this exercise completed, and before plotting the details of your proposed financial journey, it is wise to assess your basic reactions and determine if, given your financial history to date, there are behavioral patterns that would benefit from modification.

How each person reacts to changes in the economic winds and speed current depends very much on the position of the Moon at birth. If you know your time of birth, you can use one of the many free Astrology software packages to ascertain its position by sign in your birth chart.

For example, suppose that you were born when the Sun was moving through the sign of Gemini. The Moon, which travels through all twelve signs in the course of the month, could be in any one of the other signs of the zodiac. It will only be in the sign of Gemini if you were born around the time of that month's New Moon when both Sun and Moon are in the same sign. If you were born at the Full Moon then, for example, the Sun would be in Gemini and the Moon in Sagittarius.

People born with the Moon in the Fire sign of Sagittarius, but not necessarily at the Full Moon, will likely display enthusiastic reactions and perhaps show signs of wanderlust. They may be generous, be quick to spend, and talk about places they'd like to visit. If you know them well, you might also observe that they own multiple purses or wallets each with the appropriate currency for the areas of the world they plan to visit. We might wonder if they are just a little too cavalier at times and even show signs of being a spendthrift. And yes, we may be concerned about their ability to budget or to cope with crisis (sudden expenditure).

These reactions are in direct contract with people born with the Moon in the sign of Cancer. They may wonder why the Moon in Sagittarius person didn't shop around more and hold something in reserve in case of catastrophe. The individual with the Moon in Cancer would likely spend what seems to be an inordinate amount (at least to the Moon in Sagittarius person) securing their nest and keeping it in good shape. The Sagittarian Moon might wonder why this friend or colleague needs to collect so much stuff and why they don't spend more on adventures. As an observation, a Cancerian Moon position is often found in the charts of those who retain sentimentality toward their wallet, which often contains family photos and other memorabilia.

Though these are extremes, it is nevertheless true that where money is concerned, there are many, different patterns of behavior. It is certainly true too that there is a very fine line between knowing when to seize a bargain (usually requiring quick reaction) and showing financial acuity by thorough risk assessment. Some people make purchases at speed; later regretting that they didn't "shop around," while others regret having "missed opportunities."

There is more to it than just the relationship of the Sun to the Moon. Reaction is modified by the interaction of the Moon's position with other planets and indeed, how prominently it is placed in your birth chart (whether it was in the top, bottom or which side of the horoscope). It is also important to know the distance of the Moon from Earth. If you were born at perigee, then the Moon was at its closest to our planet. At apogee it was furthest away. There are two other cycles that might also be considered: declination and latitude. Each of these gives valuable clues as to your response system. All these factors would be taken into account by an experienced astrologer.

The Moon is linked to the nurturing system and its position in the birth chart says much about how we each handle family matters, our actual homes (nests), how we eat, how we save, and even how we carry money. Though it is not possible in this work to cover all the various and complex factors involved, some observations may be helpful. In Appendix 3 you will find some quick and general notes on the position of the Moon by sign.

It is also true that our financial positions are greatly affected by our closest partners. Knowing how colleagues, close partners or relatives are likely to react to cosmic weather is helpful and oftentimes results in us adjusting our financial sails if they be fellow crew members.

Plotting and Planning

Not so many centuries ago, priority was often simply to survive. The concept of saving for retirement, building a pension, etc. is relatively new—which perhaps goes some way to explaining why so many people find this difficult if not impossible to achieve. Not so many generations back, these concepts were unknown. The need to develop this financial behavior is, perhaps, not yet built into our DNA.

Unlike our ancestors, most people in the West now assume

that there will come a time when they will NOT work: either through choice or ill-health. Determining how much or when you will need to draw on resources has tested the expertise of actuaries since the idea of life insurance was first developed in the mid-nineteenth century. Complex spreadsheets are now prepared, and risk factors considered.

The content of this chapter differs from many other methods of offering financial guidance in that the aim here is to identify both potential stormy periods versus those years when sailing with the wind, picking up speed, preserving assets, and seizing opportunity is less of a challenge and, indeed, potentially exciting. You can choose to think of it this way: the position and cycles of the outer planets alert us to the "shipping lanes" offering safest travel and suggest which currents should be avoided at all cost.

Using planetary cycles as a guide to plotting your course is an ancient method. From the cradle of civilization, Mesopotamia, and across the world to ancient Mayan civilization, study of planetary cycles has yielded clues as to the optimum time to gather crops, gather harvests, and go to market. By following the stars or planets, farmers, kings and rulers made their future financial plans. Of course such plans could be blown off target by a variety of factors. These cycles though formed the basis for their future casting.

The problem of unresolved global debt and the number of governments living beyond their means should concern us all. Collapse is inevitable. This debt bubble will burst—and most probably before Pluto leaves Capricorn in 2023. Government bonds will likely NOT be repaid. The same may be true of much corporate debt. Time and care will be required to determine the solvency—or not—of both governments and companies.

Having accepted that a very dangerous undercurrent exists, and that treasury bonds and even state pensions (and perhaps other pensions) are unlikely to pay out as hoped, we need to look ahead to other options that might secure our financial future.

Though this work is not a treatise on numerology, I think we can agree that five is a special number. My suggestion is to develop five financial plans. The five digits of each hand serve as daily reminders of the plans chosen. Just as each finger is of different shape and length, so too may be your savings and financial plans. The fact that there are five does not mean that they have to be equal! What suits one person may not suit another. It would, however be wise not to have ninety percent in one plan and spread the other four plans amongst the remaining ten percent! That said, twenty percent in each, though it might appear the optimum way forward, will suit very few people. For example, if you own your own business, you might prefer to have a larger stake in maintaining its condition so that you can sell it at a later date.

Savings and Investment Strategies:

A Five Point Plan with Practical Steps to Astro-Money Management

1. Cash Reserves and Digital Currencies

The demise of cash? The world of money is most decidedly changing. Digital currencies are becoming the norm. Yet these are vulnerable to hacking, power failure, and simple theft. For now we might agree that our priority should always be to have cash—or an alternative—ready for emergency. That sounds and looks to be an easy or simple exercise but does require careful thought. For example, do you have a regular place where you keep your wallet? If there was a fire, would you be able to locate it quickly? This is such a basic step but indicative of so much more. There is comfort in knowing that you can locate this financial safety net with ease and that within that wallet or purse there will be enough cash to get you to a safe haven.

At a different level, you should also give thought to trust: do you trust your country's currency? Depending on your age and country of residence, you might recall a time when a particular bank-note was withdrawn and replaced. In many countries, higher denomination banknotes have been most vulnerable to change—but not exclusively.

Whatever cash you do choose to keep close, it's as well to check it at least quarterly and, perhaps regularly exchange saved bank notes for the type currently in use. (Twice in the recent past, colleagues passing through London have been shocked to discover banknotes they'd saved from just a few years ago were no longer in circulation and had to be exchanged at the main city bank. Not difficult but certainly an inconvenient exercise.)

Then there is the question of what kind of currency to hold. Would you prefer to hold just your own national currency, or spread risk by holding more than one kind? Much will depend on your experience and your natal chart. Broadly the rule is that if you are born under one of the Mutable signs of Gemini, Virgo, Sagittarius or Pisces, holding more than two currencies will feel "right."

Those born under the Cardinal signs of Aries, Cancer, Libra, or Capricorn could choose just two currencies with the bias toward the one with which they are most familiar. For those born under these signs, another "currency" might take the form of gold or silver coins: the point being is that there is diversification. This is less true of those born under the Fixed signs of Taurus, Leo, Scorpio, or Aquarius. This group might feel that cash reserve in their own currency is more than adequate.

Clearly these are generalizations, but that doesn't make the ideas invalid. By grouping signs together in this way, it can help focus the mind. What is important is that consideration of cash reserve is given.

There should be no suggestion that cash reserve takes the form of "notes under the mattress," though easy access is the whole point of emergency savings. This reserve should be somewhere that can be reached with physical ease: not miles away or even in another country. Depending on the actual amount in secure keeping, it might even be that this "fifth of savings" is sub-divided further into an amount kept handy in your purse or wallet, and the remainder in an easy access account.

Most of us grew up with the idea of having a "healthy bank account." While this has been true, given the challenges that lie ahead, we should all give very careful thought indeed as to which of those institutions are trustworthy.

Bear in mind that any cash kept in an account is vulnerable to electronic fraud or genuine mishap. Where possible, ensure that the amounts are within government protected limits. (In Europe, funds are presently protected up to 85K Euros).

Crypto-Currencies

As has been pointed out in another chapter, if history repeats, then money as we have known it will be radically changed—and perhaps eventually disappear in physical form. Electronic or digital cash is already in wide-spread use. At the time of writing it appears that Sweden will be the first country to offer its own crypto-currency. Already in that part of the world, cash is no longer king: the norm being for digital and mobile phone financial transactions. What happens though if for any reason the technical systems on which these are run, are put out of action?

As we have said, there is always the danger of technical systems being rendered out of action by events quite beyond human control. Should a communications satellite be unable to operate, then block chain transactions would suffer immediate breakdown with potentially catastrophic consequences.

Few people would disagree that money, or something tangible that can be bartered, will need to coexist with these developing block chain currencies so that trade can continue even if these systems fail. The big question is, of course, which of the present day currencies can be relied upon to stay in existence? Unthinkable as it may be for many, the US dollar in its present form might no longer exist; though whatever replaces it in the United States could of course have global demand.

At the time of writing, there is much discussion as to whether the US dollar will be replaced by the Chinese currency, the *remnimbi*, as the global reserve currency. It is perhaps more likely that it will be one of the new block chain currencies that assumes this role. Tempting as it is to speculate as to which of these new offerings is best placed to survive, I am not willing to advocate holding very large amounts of any crypto-currency until at least 2029, though there is a good case for having some holdings in these. Having a foothold in one or more of these crypto-currencies should be considered. The risk assessment involved in their selection will likely be complex and perhaps best left to those familiar with their development.

Over two thousand types of crypto-currencies are now in existence. Though many people are familiar with Bitcoin, Ripple, or Ethereum, they are by no means the only prominent players in this fast-developing sector. If you do choose to make a foray into this potentially lucrative market, you will need to select your crypto-currency with care—and preferably at a time when your own chart does not suggest that you are in danger of being lured onto financial rocks.

It is probable that post the Jupiter-Saturn alignment in the Air-sign of Aquarius in December 2020, crypto-currencies will be ubiquitous. While those with Pluto in Leo (1939–1956) could find this a challenge, those born later will most likely have accepted that these currencies are here to stay and are a necessary part of a cash portfolio—though all should be aware of the potential for misadventure. For example, Uranus (planet of the unexpected) arrives at the midpoint of these two planets in January 2021, and on several occasions in 2023, there are danger signals ahead.

It's in 2029—and just ahead of an important alignment of Saturn and Uranus, that initial difficulties associated with block-chain technology should abate. Though it is true that these currencies will always be susceptible to collapse through solar or other cosmic disturbance, it will surely be important to most people to have some holdings in this sector.

Speculators might like to make a foray into this area before Uranus arrives in Gemini (fast currency transactions) in July 2025. That planet then moves to make strong and positive aspect to Pluto with the inference that crypto-currencies will gain fast traction. For most people, however, it will surely be advisable to wait until closer to the end of the next decade before building reserves in digital currencies—and only after determining which of the many on offer then have proven management behind them.

For the present, priority will surely be given to local currency and perhaps that of neighboring regions—or the currency of the nation where we have friends or relatives. In the US, some may choose to hold amounts in Canadian dollars or Mexico pesos. In the UK, holding Euros may be more attractive, while in Australia or New Zealand, there may be usefulness in holding a little in the other currency.

Generally, in planning your personal year ahead, most of us factor in a holiday. Buying appropriate currency for the regions to be visited makes sense). Some might only dream of visiting far flung places. But even these dreams may be realized under fortunate transits.

Consider those years when Jupiter is making passage through your sun sign (Jupiter will make this transit for roughly one year in every twelve. It is entirely possible that in those years you might wish to spread your wings and visit far-flung places. Before doing so, it might be helpful to have some local cash available. (A list of Jupiter's transits through the twelve signs in given in Appendix 4)

As you are no doubt aware, there are various ways in which to acquire currency. The most costly is buying at the last minute at the airport. Preplanning is generally more financially astute. Though for most people, the amount involved is not huge, it is nevertheless wise to keep an eye on fluctuating rates. Familiarizing yourself with these fluctuations, and being able to calculate the true price of items and products in another currency, can be either an exasperating or enjoyable exercise!

The general rule is to try to avoid doing foreign exchange on days either side of Mercury (the planet of commerce) appearing to move into either retrograde or direct motion. Volatility can be pronounced on these occasions. A list of Mercury's stations is given in Appendix 5.

2: Property

As one of the five components of an investment strategy, property might seem an unrealistic aim for some. Yet property covers more than just a place to live and includes all items whose value could be realized through sale. These are CHOSEN investments: most people buy an item because they like it. Unless they are truly weird, it's probable that someone else will like it too and be willing to pay to own it. Most of us own something that has value.

Most obviously there is the property in which you reside. This is a major investment for many people and certainly it is easy to view home ownership as a form of security. Few achieve that security until it is fully paid for, of course. Until the mortgage is redeemed, the property is not rightfully "yours."

Even then, and before assuming that it will hold value, it is necessary to review where that property is situated. For example: might it be in the path of a hurricane? Yes, even home ownership does not guarantee that you won't be faced with a property asset crisis at some stage. That said, investing in bricks and mortar, and thus not having the liability of renting in old age, is arguably a sound investment.

I would caution against viewing a home as something from which equity can be released. Though this has become a favored system by those who have no wish to downsize from one property to another, it is not a good option for everyone. It can also be super expensive and the costs of equity withdrawal outrageously high.

In my client work so far, the only people who have toyed with this option have been born with the Sun in Aries or Gemini. (Please note that the sample size is ridiculously small. That said, it seems "right" that these two signs would put forward the case for this action: Aries because it offers a quick fix, and Gemini because being on the move offers excitement). I have yet to hear of a Cancer or Capricorn giving this serious thought!

At the very least, money should always be set aside to maintain the good repair of your nest. This occasionally requires more than routine maintenance: it may be necessary to adapt your home to different needs as you age. Here, even a rudimentary understanding of planetary positions is helpful. Though the position of all the planets would be considered by an experienced astrologer, much information can be gained from working with Saturn's position by sign alone. (Appendix 6)

Consider: we are aware that as Saturn travels through our

Sun sign—a transit that lasts for roughly 30 months every 30 years, bones tend to creak and we "feel our age." Should this period coincide with a time when we might expect our bones to weaken (perhaps over age 70), we might reasonably wonder if we need to make adjustment to our homes to enable ease of movement (hand-rails, different handles, etc.). Budgeting for these and, perhaps for hearing aids or extra glasses etc. should be seen as wise. Obviously it would also be wise to carry out repairs when the cost of doing so is within budget. In recent times even financial advisors, who rarely mentioned such planning, have suggested that home upkeep be given particular attention in the years leading up to retirement. My experience has been that these tasks are more comfortably approached after the usual retirement age (65) and before age 72.

Give thought too to the age of your property. Homes—like people—experienced Saturn Returns (around age 30, 56, 85, and 115). In the case of my own home, at age 115 it required a major refit. That this occurred during a period when we could afford to give the house the attention it deserved was fortunate. At the previous Saturn return, the situation was very different. Repairs and adjustments made under tight constraints at that time required urgent re-investment at Saturn's half-return, fifteen years later.

As you will know, your horoscope is drawn as a circle. The base of the chart (found at the 6 o'clock point) can be viewed as a property point. Note that the sign at this base does not have to be the same as the Sun sign under which you were born (that is only true if you were born in the middle of the night). Again, if you haven't already obtained a copy of your birth chart, there are various websites offering this free service.

Saturn will pass the base point of a horoscope roughly every 30 years. It is often the case that this marks a period when the individual puts down roots—sometimes in the form of a house purchase. This same transit can also coincide with many other events. It does seem to be a time when most people give thought to domestic concerns and when property is viewed as a desirable asset. Saturn's arrival at the square and oppositions to this point (roughly 7 and 14 years later) should also be viewed as potentially active asset management periods.

Property as Investment:

For some people, property has proved a sound investment. There are downsides: property requires maintenance. Even if in a position to earn income through rental, not all that rent will be yours. There will be expenses: insurance, local taxes, repair, agents' fees, and an allowance for the time when the property isn't occupied.

Rental trends vary according to location. Careful study of past trends, together with a review of the chart for the city in question, is useful. For example, rents in London between 2011 and 2017 rose by twenty-three percent—clearly an excellent return. House prices rose even higher. The chart for London reflects this probability but also shows the likelihood of a downturn from late 2018. Given that in recent years, property has been a form of currency in this and other major capital cities, it is perhaps not surprising that during the difficulties to be faced as the great stellium forms in Capricorn in 2020, there will be massive re-evaluation of the "bricks and mortar" values of homes and commercial buildings in these centers.

Obtaining the chart of a city is neither as hard nor as strange as it sounds. Most have dates of incorporation or other significant documentation. That of Washington DC, March 15, 1791 at 16:12 local time is most interesting. In this chart, the Moon is placed in home-loving Cancer. Home-loving does not always mean expensive, and Washington DC certainly has its fair share of both super-expensive homes and impoverished ones. Re-evaluation of their values is probable as Pluto opposes the Moon in this chart in 2023–2024. Through these years some may find it too expensive to stay in that city, whereas others may endure the pain of knowing that their much-loved homes are losing considerable value.

Owning more than one property has another potential

downside—especially as Pluto completes its journey through Capricorn in 2023. Given the difficulties governments will have to face to pay off debts, they may choose to increase or put in place property taxes for second-home owners. This is a very real possibility through 2019 and 2020 when first Jupiter and then Saturn join Pluto in Capricorn. The lunar node will also be moving through property-associated Cancer. The total effect suggests pressure on homeowners and yes, for some, the specter of negative equity. Those in the fortunate position of owning their home free of debt should try and stay that way.

Not everyone will own—or even desire to own their own home of course. In some parts of the world, home ownership is rare. In these instances, priority may be given to items that have long-lasting value and which are intended to be passed on to heirs. Asset classes include works of art, rare books or other artefacts.

Art as Investment and Enjoyment

Pleasure is a factor that should be considered as you plan. Being surrounded by beauty has a positive effect on the soul. Whether this takes the form of buying a soap whose scent brings pleasure, or a painting that offers moments of quiet contemplation, there are myriad ways in which to make investment: temporary or long-term. While the purchase of soap for immediate use brings fleeting pleasure, a work of art can bring daily joy and, at some point be exchanged for another item (cash, item, or needed service).

The price of anything is only what someone is willing to pay for it. Valuations and estimates are exceedingly hard to determine. Investing in art should not form the core of a portfolio. There are inherent risks: what is popular in one period may be of little value in another.

Few people have the experience of selling works of art, but many of us do have experience of building collections. These will have value to someone—but are not to be relied on as investment for old age. These items should be considered more as heirlooms: emotional investments that can be passed on.

3. Self-Investment and Making Money

Self-investment is rarely discussed by a financial advisor who will tend to focus on investing in pensions, companies, property, bonds, or insurance. Self-investing is a very different area altogether. There are, of course, a myriad of ways in which to deploy this task: from investing in your interests, or your own business, to choosing stocks without the aid of an expert.

Tempting as it is to invest in the hope that through other people's expertise, cash can be made (through investment in shares)—it is always good to review areas in which you at least feel you have some control. Assuming there are no major health issues. It is surely wise to invest in skills and talents that could be sold or bartered and which may not be age-dependent, or in stocks related to products and services with which you feel to have some affinity. Notes on choosing stocks are given in the final chapter where we prepare for Full Steam Ahead.

Even if you have spent your entire working life in an area that is now redundant (which will be the case for many who have worked in manufacturing, for example, or whose tasks may well be undertaken by robots in the future), it would be wise not to underestimate the value of the reliability shown during employment. In joining teams working in new areas, that earlier experience will surely prove invaluable—and have its own premium. Once Pluto begins its journey through Aquarius, those who know how to work in cooperation with others—and maybe even with robots!—will surely find their presence welcomed and rewarded.

Having "something to do" is essential for general well-being. If that something can also be bartered for other goods and services or financial reward, then so much the better. Some people are better at negotiating than others. Though all signs will likely recognize the need to tap into underlying entrepreneurial talents as Uranus makes its way through Taurus (2018–2025), those born under the Fixed signs of Taurus, Leo, Scorpio or Aquarius will likely be most aware of these traits surfacing. Going off to "do their own thing" will likely be a driving force.

Uranus—the driver where developing a unique selling point is concerned—was identified in 1781 not by an astronomer, but by a musician, who was a part-time but very enthusiastic amateur astronomer. The very nature of its discovery and the person who found it describes almost exactly one of the traits associated with that planet: desire. Until 1781, Saturn, the last of the solar system planets that can be seen with the naked eye, seemed to mark a boundary. With the discovery of Uranus, the possibility of the solar system being bigger—far, far bigger—than previously thought was, to many, a mind-blowing discovery. It should come as no surprise that William Herschel was feted in the streets and lauded by the King. His was an exceptional life journey, neatly encapsulating the pursuit of a dream and the applause realized when achievement is made.

The circumstances of Uranus' discovery are reflected in the way in which it is considered to correlate to human behavior. Uranus is the planet of the unexpected, the planet that requires things to be done differently, and, at those times when it takes up a prominent position in the skies, coincides with surprising developments. It is associated with non-conformity, with rebelliousness, driven temperament, and single-mindedness.

We all have Uranus somewhere in our charts, so all have at least some potential as entrepreneurs. A few of us might show this trait while still at school—though the surfacing of desire has the potential to get people into trouble if it contravenes existing rules. For others, latent talent may not come out until the "chips are down," surprising even the individuals themselves with their flair and commitment: gifts they never thought they had or could put to good use.

As Uranus moves through Taurus (2018–2024) we should expect those born under the Fixed signs (listed above) to be more determined, more single-minded, and yes, given that entrepreneurship requires these qualities, most likely to break away and to "do their own thing." Given the probability of some of these ideas being ahead of their time, they may well tune in to wants, needs and desires in services and goods that have yet to develop mass appeal.

Uranus' Taurus odyssey will affect us all: igniting desires that become increasingly compelling. Amongst these may well be the desire for craftsmanship. If you are of an age when you could still learn or develop latent crafting talents, you may find that you can develop an earnings stream; though running any business requires many and complex skills to achieve success.

It is arguably the case that those born with Pluto in Virgo (born 1956–1972) are best placed to develop crafting skills before 2023, and, assuming that they do have the necessary latent business skills, to develop a second revenue stream through this investment.

This not to say that those with Pluto in Leo (1939–1956) or Libra (1972–1984) can't also develop new revenue streams. Given their age and talents, in their different ways, they could yet make the most of Uranus' transit of Taurus and explore new avenues for reward.

Those least well placed to develop revenue streams before 2023–2024 are arguably those born a little later with Pluto in Scorpio or Sagittarius. These individuals might not have either the connections or capital to get a new scheme off the ground.

It may be a statement of the obvious, but money does not grow on trees! Until a product or service is launched and gathers its own momentum—at which point you might be able to retire and simply watch profits drop into your account—energy is required. Priority then must be given to health. If you're in the unfortunate position of being lacking in this area, you should give well-being your full attention before you turn your mind to realizing financial reward for other efforts. This is not to say that you can't plan in the interim. It can't be said often enough that money flows most easily when you are doing something that you enjoy. Under these conditions, you may put in well more than the required hundred percent of effort or 100,000 hours of commitment and with that added value, make a name for yourself and develop a demand for your services.

Assuming that you are in good health and that you have the germ of an idea, the next and practical step is not necessarily to develop a full business plan but to make a simple statement of intent. What is the product or service? Why would anyone want it? Is there competition? What could you do to make your offering the preferred choice? This conceptual task should never be overlooked. The clearer you are about your aims and objectives, the more likely they are to be realized.

Breaks in even the darkest of cosmic financial clouds do occur. It clearly makes most sense to launch a new business when as many planets as possible are in direct motion as viewed from Earth. Those periods are not always easy to find. Arguably the toughest time to launch and make success of an enterprise is when many planets are in retrograde motion. Avoiding those times when four or more planets are retrograde is to be recommended.

It is also wise to avoid a launch in the two days before the New Moon and arguably the day after it as well. The energy through those periods is useful for incubating ideas and identifying new goals, but generally not so good for launches, which are later found to be ill-prepared.

The launch of any product or service requires huge reserves of energy. For this reason, it's wise to have Mars in direct motion. If launched under a retrograde Mars, you may find that you are either undercapitalized, lack sufficient expertise, or the right number of staff and assistance to make progress.

These are, of course, not the only factors that would be taken into consideration by an experienced astrologer. But the comments do, however, offer a rough and ready guide.

The key factor here is that a third part of your portfolio should be focused on YOU. It might be a small part, but factoring this in at whatever level, should be viewed as a key element in your long-term financial planning.

4. Commodities

Many people unknowingly invest in these through their pension plans. Yet you can invest directly. Those who do venture into this area tend to focus on just one commodity: very often gold or gold coins or silver or other precious metals or stones. Still others choose to invest in what are known as Exchange Traded Finds

(ETFs) where there is no need for you to own the physical gold but instead are part of a community of like-minded investors)

If you are new to this type of investment, there are a few points to note:

Soft commodities are agricultural products such as wheat, coffee, cocoa, fruit and sugar. Hard commodities include anything that is mined, e.g., gold and oil. Soft commodities are clearly more weather dependent. They are also susceptible to disease and pestilence. Obviously, before investing in soft commodities there is much to learn. You likely need to understand optimum growing and trading conditions, but, given that these soft commodities have been traded for many years (centuries even), you will not be short of research material.

From the astrological perspective, it is possible to identify years when harvests are likely to be poor or ruined by using ancient astrological "weather techniques." When certain aspects between planets form during the planting season, there is greater likelihood of these crops being damaged through flood. Using one of these techniques indicates that in the USA, the years 2019, 2023, 2027, and 2033 will likely see flooding of the Mississippi basin with subsequent loss of crops. For farmers this is devastating. Consumers too will find that shortage of available harvested crops leads to increased prices on supermarket shelves. The years given then may be ones to avoid if you choose to consider investing in these crops.

Hard commodities attract much attention. Many people like the idea of owning gold or other precious metals. This of course carries risk: gold, silver, jewels, etc. need protection. Exactly where are you going to keep these investments? Or are you going to pay someone to look after them for you? Some companies offer this service—but at a price. Fact is that ownership will entail security costs.

The next question is "when to buy." Given the high probability of commercial turbulence, it is likely wise to buy before a possible peak in precious metal prices in March 2020. The next super-peak in gold prices may be in 2038.

There are different types of traders: those who buy and sell within hours (day traders), those who trade regularly (perhaps monthly), irregular traders (when the mood takes them), and those who play for the long term. With the latter and where gold is concerned, prices may be low in 2025–2026. Tying up money for 12–13 years on the basis that the price might rise in 2038, is not a suitable strategy for those who may need access to profits in the interim.

For those who are happy to buy and sell at least annually and using planetary cycles, the first thing to remember is that it is imperative to follow your own chart. If you are under difficult aspects, it is wise not to buy or sell anything unless under the guidance of an experienced trader who could, at the very least, prevent great loss.

Assuming though that you are not under dark cosmic clouds, and that you have undertaken adequate risk assessment, you could choose to buy gold a month ahead of each Mars-Jupiter geocentric conjunction and sell the day before that cosmic event. You won't catch either the exact top or bottom, but, if the past is any indicator of the future, you could make significant gain. See Appendix 7 for these dates.

A precious metal of particular interest to me is platinum which experienced two major highs in the last fifty years: on both occasions when there was significant planetary activity in Aquarius. With Jupiter and Saturn forming their next conjunction in this sign, and periods when the inner planets and Sun will join them in Aquarius, it is probable that a new high will be reached in February 2021. Those who by then may be wary of equities (that will likely have lost ground), and unsure even then of cash currencies, may be drawn toward precious metals, whose value though could be quickly lost. The optimum time for purchase may be while Jupiter is still in Capricorn (i.e. before December 20, 2020) with a view to selling before the end of January 2021. Yes, this is a short period: less than a month. It could nevertheless bring a boost to savings. While at the time of writing the risk does not seem great, it will, of course, be essential to apply technical analysis and take advice from a financial advisor before making any purchase.

From the astro-perspective, silver should always be considered as part of your portfolio. Its uses are widespread and demand likely to be high as the technical age gathers even greater momentum. It is already in great demand within the field of medicine and if, as I suspect, that health will be a dominating theme in the next decade, then reasonable to expect demand for this metal to rise.

It is very interesting that in the space of less than 30 months following the global financial crash in 2008, the silver index moved from a low of $9.20 to a high of $48 in April 2011. By the end of that year the index was at $27. Clearly this is a volatile commodity and trading should be undertaken with the assistance of an expert.

That expert might be more than a little interested in the effect of lunar cycles on this index. To be specific, turning points are often reached when the Moon's perigee or apogee coincides with a lunar phase (New, First, Full, or Last Quarter). This in itself does not pinpoint the years in which this index should see great growth but is still worthy of consideration alongside other factors.

In 2011, when the index reached $48, Mercury, Venus, Mars, and Jupiter were all in Aries. Jupiter will reach this area of the zodiac again in December 2022. At the end of March 2023, Mercury and Venus will join both the Sun and Jupiter in Aries. If we then take the lunar perigee and apogee into consideration, we might wonder if another high will be reached. Please note: this is still insufficient information with which to trade, but, if confirmed by technical analysis, may be valuable.

Other precious jewels (easily transported) should also be considered. It is arguably as wise to have a collection of jewelry that can be traded and enjoyed while owned, rather than have cash in a bank that may or may not be safe.

5. Equities

This is arguably the main area where people think that knowledge of planetary placement will give them the edge. Yet there are literally thousands and thousands of companies to choose from and as many charts to consider. Determining which will outperform the market is in one sense a little like looking for a needle in a haystack. However, having equities as part of your investment portfolio is advisable. Even if you think you know nothing about shares and how they are traded, there is high probability that already you do have a stake in these through pensions and savings. The advisers of those institutions will have invested in equities on your behalf.

It can be an enjoyable exercise to make your own choices however. From choosing so-called penny shares to investing in a long-established businesses with much higher share price, the process of selection, although apparently daunting, is perhaps not quite as difficult as you think. It also permits ethical and philanthropic considerations that might not be the choice of institutional investors.

It is salutary to look at the charts of fund managers, i.e. investors with large portfolios of shares, who have been successful. Their birthdate is sometimes listed when they are profiled in newspapers. Again, you would need to look at this with your astrologer. The exercise can be worthwhile! Even without this birth information, you know that their success is built on a mixture of experience, knowledge, and gut instinct. Experience, of course, only comes through time. Knowledge can certainly be acquired. Gut instinct you already have. In short, all that may be missing from this part of your portfolio is application.

If you've never invested before, it is arguably wise to choose those companies and services that you yourself use. As has been said earlier in this work, unless you are highly unusual, if you are using a product or service, then the chances are that others will be doing so too. Also having in your portfolio shares in long-established businesses which have a good track record of paying dividends is always wise.

Previous chapters should have given you an idea of the sectors likely to advance and their probable periods of growth. It does not however assist you in selecting the companies themselves. As explained, there are thousands if not millions of these. This work cannot possibly cover even a fraction of those seeking investment.

There are however, some superb astrologers (notably Grace Morris in Chicago), who observes the dates of IPOs and offers investment advice based on the positions of the planets at IPO. Key dates are those when the Sun and Jupiter are positively aligned, for which, please see Appendix 8. It would be wholly insufficient to purchase shares on the basis of this information alone, and imperative to examine the fundamentals of the company and the position of other planets in its chart. However, with such information, combined with listening to your gut instinct, making your choice ought not to be too difficult.

Yet you can look out of this box. Look around you. It's not impossible that you will see an item or service with great promise. For example, you may have no intention of ever going skateboarding but might recognize it as a growing craze. Find out more. Certainly, find out more about the companies making these products, their "birth date," and consider how well that works with your own.

We would all of course like to find the next Microsoft or Google or Apple and get in on the ground floor of a similar enterprise. Yet there are other businesses offering potential profit. Understanding planetary cycles alerts us to the sectors likely to thrive in a given period.

Futuristic trends are often indicated by Uranus' position. This planet takes approximately eighty-four years to travel through all twelve signs spending roughly about seven years in each sign. Through the better part of the first decade of the millennium that planet was moving through the sign of Aquarius. This is when technologies captured the imagination and when Microsoft, Apple, and Google shares soared.

Uranus then moved into the sign of Pisces; the sign associated with pharmaceuticals, film, and media. Developments in all of these areas have seen those companies grow and return good profit in recent years.

Uranus then moved on into Aries and cosmic attention

turned to those businesses deemed to be "at the cutting edge": often embracing military hardware, but also advanced robotic technology. Drones, which a few years ago were unheard of, are now in regular use and the businesses providing these are doing well. It is unlikely that those who invested in these enterprises will be disappointed with returns.

Uranus has recently moved into the sign of Taurus and will leave that sign in 2025. Industries set to move quickly and to advance by benefiting from new technologies between now and then include farming and agriculture. Taurus is the first of the Earth signs of the Zodiac. Of course, farming and agriculture require support from many other industries. If we consider those which benefited as Uranus moved through Aries (which includes of course the drone technology) we will likely see this applied to farming methods. It is perhaps not too late to invest in these areas.

If however, you are looking for something rather more long-term and most decidedly want to benefit from getting in on the ground floor now, you'd arguably do well to focus on those industries that will take off at speed once Uranus reaches Gemini. This could be literal. From 2025 through until 2032 should be the era of the smart or electronic car.

These same years should see the real growth of robotic technology. Though advances here will make many people redundant, companies building and providing supporting technology should do very well indeed.

In discussion with a colleague it was suggested that I conclude this chapter by addressing the issue of "what to do when you've forgotten how to make money": aptly describing moments in most people's life journeys when an individual feels financially marooned.

The probability is that this situation is temporary. The planets do not stand still and conditions change. Focus must be on being alert to even subtle changes in the cosmic weather patterns and not being "asleep at the wheel." Remain ready to take advantage of prevailing winds again!

Your astrologer can help you do this. Even without that assistance, know that there will be market changes at each phase of the Moon. There is no cost to finding out when that will be. Look up at the night sky. There is an old adage that turning over a coin at the Full Moon will assist in changing your financial fortunes.

Being marooned or becalmed is not a good experience but neither is being subjected to pestilence or disease. In this next chapter we will consider other difficulties that may be faced as you navigate the financial seas.

CHAPTER 3

Vermin, Risk Assessment, and Insurance

Rodents on board a ship are not uncommon. Even today, pests (from bed-bugs to other unwelcome critters) have the potential to spoil a trip. Provisions are damaged and goods destroyed, while passengers and crew alike may experience disease through infestation or food poisoning. Whatever the attempts are to prevent these occurrences, risk of these is recognized and offset by putting travel and liability insurance in place. Even so, it is essential for staff and passengers to carry out regular risk-management exercises and, where appropriate, take steps to mitigate the effect of such incidents.

This chapter looks at the cosmic signatures for financial "pests" and when these might appear during our journey.

Vermin and Pestilence and Health Checks: Financial and Physical

Of course we should assume that you are ready for the voyage ahead. Even so, it's still possible that there is a rat or disease onboard. A meeting with your Chief Medical Officer (financial advisor) is advisable before you set sail. Yes, this will take time and yes, it could be expensive. It would, however, surely be wise.

As you read this, do you have any idea of your financial position? Take time to note down what you have in your wallet, various accounts, and the nominal value of items. From this next deduct any debts. Having even a rough and ready idea of where you are financially is not intended to be a worrying exercise. But it will give you an idea of your base position.

Before moving ahead, and just as your financial health requires regular maintenance, so too should be your physical health. Again, it's wise to choose a time of year to do this. Non-astrologers could mark these essential visits in their diaries for the month ahead of their birthdays. If you know your birth chart well, you might consider those periods in the year when the Sun passes through the fifth or eleventh houses of your natal chart. That might not be the advice you expected, since health matters are generally given over to the sixth and eighth houses of the horoscope. But choosing months ahead of these transits, any treatment can be done as the Sun moves from the fifth to sixth or from the eleventh to the twelfth.

Of course you should also check your provision situation and think carefully about the diet that will be needed in the coming years. Don't lose sight of the fact that what you need today—in terms of vitamin and minerals—today may well change during the voyage. It might help to draw up a health budget. There is also health insurance to consider. While insurance is an essential, as important is a sound support system: friends and family, should you need extra care.

There are, of course, diseases over which you might have very little control. It is now several years since there was a pandemic. Many feel that this is overdue. While there have been the scares of bird flu, Sars and the Ebola virus, these have been much contained. There has, as yet, been no repeat of the so-called "Spanish" flu that was a major factor in bringing World War I to a close.

From biblical times there have been plagues and diseases that have culled large sectors of the population. Certain areas of the world have been decimated by smallpox, measles, and yellow fever, while other locations remained unaffected. In today's world with travel so easy, contagion is a very real possibility. Germs can travel literally thousands of miles within a few hours. An infected person might not even show symptoms of a disease during his or her flight, and so unwittingly infect others.

From the Bubonic plague and Black Death through to the Spanish Flu, Aids, and Ebola, there is correlation between planetary position and the outbreak of disease. The planetary "signatures" of each vary hugely though a common one concerns the relationship of Pluto to the planetoid Chiron. This planetary picture was apparent during the cholera outbreak at the dawn of the twentieth century, and formed again in 1917–1918 at the onset of the Spanish Flu contagion at the end of World War I.

Over 350 million people were infected by that flu virus, between 30 and 50 million died as a result. By contrast, World War brought the deaths of seven million civilians and 10 million military personnel.

A quick review of the diseases of the last thousand years reveals few periods when humans have not had to deal with widespread infection and disease. There have been whole centuries when epidemics have rolled one after the other across different continents. It is of interest that the start of each appears to have had one common planetary signature: a major aspect between Pluto and Chiron.

Until 2023, Pluto moves through Capricorn. In April 2018, Chiron arrives in another of the Cardinal signs, Aries. Though those two signs form a natural square to one another, Pluto and Chiron will not form this exact square aspect with one another as they move through these signs. They do, however, form an arguably more significant aspect, a quintile, in February 2020.

As has already been noted, 2020 promises to be an exceptional year on the world financial stage with tough measures severely restricting growth. Should there also be a pandemic at the same time, it would create extraordinary difficulty. While pharmaceutical companies and bio-technologies should find that their share prices rise—as might those businesses providing daily health care and, after loss of life, funeral care—others may be more concerned with simple survival.

Lending strength to the possibility of a pandemic, another orbiting body revisits an area of the zodiac for the first time since the seventeenth century. A group of planetary bodies orbiting beyond Pluto—whose presence has been mathematically calculated but which have yet to be seen and verified by astronomers—are known as the Trans-Neptunians. They include Hades (associated with death).

Most astro-software programs will calculate these positions. As they orbit so far away from the Sun, the orbits of the Trans-Neptunians are very long indeed. Between 1655 and 1685—so covering the years of the Great Plague or Black Death in London and in Vienna—the Trans-Neptunian planetoid Hades moved through the sign of Cancer. Hades arrived in that sign again in 2011 and won't leave Cancer until 2041. By itself this does not lead to a forecast of twenty-first century Black Death, though it may be that a long-dormant disease threatens. We should perhaps be most concerned about the period 2020–2022, when Chiron will be at apparent right angle to Hades—just as they were in 1917.

These two planetary bodies were in hard angle to one another again in 1955. A year later, the Asian flu was gaining ground eventually killing thousands. They reached their quarter phase in 1994 coinciding with a plague epidemic in Surat, India; while their opposition (exact in December 2000) coincided with both Dengue fever and the onslaught of the SARS virus.

It is not unreasonable to suspect that at their next quarter phase in 2020–2022, there will be global concern about another—as yet unnamed—virus. While it may not be possible to either avoid this infection—as it may be air or water born—it is probable that much money will be spent in an attempt to avoid being diseased or even dying from it. Protecting oneself from this event may not be possible though it is surely wise to take steps to minimize risk.

Even without a pandemic, we are all now aware that cases of Alzheimer's, dementia, and other neurological complaints are on the rise. Investment in research for cures is likely insufficient. Though most governments recognize the rise in the numbers of people at risk from these diseases, they do not yet seem ready to give adequate funding to finding cures. It is left to the pharmaceutical industry. When suitable drugs to combat such diseases are found, the cost of their provision will surely be enormous. Factoring in how one might pay for such care—either for oneself or a loved one—when the costs will surely balloon offers an enormous challenge.

Health and other insurance is certainly advisable, yet costs here will also likely soar rendering this option beyond the reach of many people. There are different elements to take into account: the cost of drugs and surgery and of actual care. While hospital care might be increasingly unaffordable for many people, the same is perhaps not true of care that is non-surgical, and perhaps not even drug dependent.

One area that might well see huge growth and development will be for sanctuary, convalescent respite, and spa care. Such concepts offer an investment opportunity with real growth potential in 2022 as Jupiter moves through the Water sign of Pisces, and again in 2030 as Jupiter moves through Scorpio.

Pest control leads to consideration of investment in these areas of potential growth: insurance inspection. There is a good case for suggesting that some hours be invested every month into reading research papers and determining dietary changes that could boost health.

Vermin and Mercury

Vigilance is, of course, the key. We all know the importance of keeping things clean, and the value of scheduling both regular cleaning and annually reviewing protection and insurance needs. We also know that there are certain essential services that must be factored into regular financial management. Paying for these should be a vital part of our regular budgeting.

Identifying the periods when an individual is most likely to experience "financial pestilence," is more easily done when we have the full natal chart (requiring date, time, and place of birth). Yet, it is still possible to identify general periods of financial irritation without this information.

The key planet here is Mercury. Its regular retrograde periods form an intricate pattern over a period of ten years. This decade-long cycle is of great interest to traders and has been a factor in determining whether or not a year is likely to be "good" or "bad" using just the numerical value of the year. For example, it is noted that during years ending in a "5," US indices have risen. This links back to the inauguration of the Dow Jones Index in 1885. Every ten years since then, as Mercury reflects the position at rgw birth of the Dow, trade on this index results in a positive finish to the year.

Mercury, the "winged messenger," the "planet of commerce." Whether it be ideas, items or services, Mercury is the planet of trade. As this planet orbits the Sun it has a "now you see me, now you don't" quality about it. As far as is known, it is the planet closest to the Sun, revolving around our special star every eighty-eight days. This number is very close indeed to the ninety day periods recognized by traders as bringing change in trend—though this is more closely connected with the Sun's apparent journey around the Earth and the marking of the seasons. Dates when Mercury reaches a Cardinal point are often days of busy trading, though those days do not always mean a change of market direction. For changes in market patterns, we will look at dates when the Sun and Mercury conjoin (as viewed from Earth). These often mark distinct changes in commercial tempo. You might even wonder if it is on one of these dates that a problem may arise that will inflict damage on provisions.

Mercury is retrograde for three periods in any year. That means, as viewed from Earth, there are three occasions in any twelve month period when Mercury appears to stand still before appearing to move backwards across the sky. After a couple of weeks of this apparent backward motion, Mercury then "stands still" once more (its direct station) before moving forward. It eventually returns to the initial degree from which it retrograded (the period between the direct station and its return to the retrograde degree is known as its "shadow"). This "loop" in the sky highlights different areas of the zodiac. It is more than a little interesting that business sectors connected to each of these highlighted areas are often in the headlines during the retrograde and its shadow period—very often experiencing "bad" publicity which occasionally affects their share price.

Traders' forecasting would be much improved if they noted Mercury's retrograde position by element (Fire, Earth, Air, or Water). Mercury does not conveniently move from one retrograde element series to another as of January 1 of each year. Taking into account the element in which retrograde Mercury periods occur would make very real difference to a trader's view of the year ahead.

Of course, pestilence of one form or another may be found at any time of the year. Whether Mercury is in direct or retrograde motion, the risk is always there. Yet it is noticeable that when

Mercury IS retrograde, financial irritations are more obvious and often prove more costly.

These retrograde periods do have a very definite pattern. A sequence is discernible with retrogrades forming in one element (Fire, Earth, Air, or Water) and then moving on to another— though occasionally the sequence is broken by a "taster" of the new element to come.

Mercury's cycle alone yields insufficient information as to when "rats" and "pestilence" might be experienced either by a whole nation or at a personal level. That planet's relationship with the Sun and with the Lunar Node gives important clues too. Before bringing these cosmic factors together, we must look closely at the pattern of Mercury's retrograde motion.

The Lunar Node and Retrograde Mercury: Commercial Twists and Turns: Potential Infection

Many of us recall the tumultuous trading conditions that are now referred to as the "Dot-Com" crash. This began in March 2000. By its end, in October 2002, the NASDAQ had lost over 78% of its value. Though there had been concern about a Millennium Bug creating commercial mayhem, astrologers had little fear of this. But we did have concern about May 2000, when several slow moving planets would be at right angles to one another. This implied a sharp change of direction that would likely be most noticeable in the market place.

While the alignment was exact during May 2000, financial astrologers involved in frequent trading were factoring in Mercury's position in order to determine optimum dates for profitable trades, while also noting the sign in which the Moon's Node was positioned.

In the 1930s, the financial astrologer Louise McWhirter noted that in the United States of America, share prices tend to rise as the Lunar Node moved from Aquarius to Leo and fall in the other half of the cycle as the Node moved back to Aquarius. (Note that the lunar node travels backwards through the zodiac over a period of approximately 18.6 years—and yes, that is not dissimilar to a recognized 20 year business cycle).

The position of the Lunar Node also indicates Solar and Lunar eclipse positions by sign. This too yields useful market-timing information.

In May 2000, the Lunar Node had just arrived in Cancer. By the time the dot-com crash was deemed to be "over" in October 2002, the Lunar Node was midway through Gemini and on the downward curve of this cycle. While decline in dot-com stocks was apparently arrested that month, the accent then shifted to other sectors—where prices continued to fall until they reached a low as the Lunar Node arrived in Aquarius in 2007, coinciding with the global financial crisis.

At the time of writing (October 2018), the Lunar Node is once again in Cancer (echoing May 2000). If history repeats itself, then once a negative trend takes hold, it will likely not be arrested until after the Node leaves Aquarius in March 2028.

While this information is interesting (incidentally suggesting that having cash available to buy into equities at likely lows in 2027–2028 would be a good long-term plan), those who want to trade more frequently require other information. Specifically they need to know the danger or optimal dates each year when they might need to take action against marauding pests.

As viewed from Earth, Mercury sometimes appears to cross the face of the Sun; a Transit of Mercury.* This event happens infrequently but, in the past has coincided with financial matters dominating news headlines, either on the day of the transit itself or within a week of it. Note that this event can only occur when Mercury is passing through either Taurus or Scorpio: the two signs often associated with banking and high finance. That the "winged messenger" should command the daily news at such

---

* Both Mercury and Venus are closer to the Sun than Earth. As viewed from Earth—and if either of these two planets are close to the ecliptic (the Sun's apparent path around us)—either will appear as a small dot crossing the face of the Sun. Presently a Mercury transit can only occur in either May or November and only if Mercury passes between the Sun and Earth.

times ought not to surprises us. From scandalous insider dealing, to adjustments in oil price that reverberate across markets to trade deals, each transit of Mercury in the twentieth century brought with it commercial events that moved markets. The next such event is due on November 11, 2019 and the one after that, on November 13, 2032.

The signs involved matter, but so too does the elemental sequence of Mercury's retrograde periods.

Elemental Matters

In 2000, each Mercury retrograde station was in a Water sign. The element is important in that this gives clues as to the kind of difficulty likely to be experienced, and so gives clues as to which market sectors will be most keenly affected. That the financial dramas of the early years of the Millennium coincided with the Moon's Node moving through another of the Water signs amplified the effect and led to crisis.

As we shall see, the combination of Mercury retrograde as the Lunar Node moves through the same element, has, in the recent past, seen strong moves in market indices. This can be a potentially overpowering wave that at the very least alters the trajectory of indices. Please note, that this is not always to the downside, but rather indicative of a great swell of activity that sees markets move more than ten percent within twelve months. Sometimes this becomes a correction, at others an upward and seductive surge.

Seven years after the dot-com crash, in September 2007, as trust in the financial system broke down and global financial collapse was openly discussed, Mercury retrogrades were again in Water signs. The Lunar Node moved through Water-sign Pisces (another Water sign) and crossed into Air-sign Aquarius, where it reached the McWhirter low point. Mercury retrogrades were again in Water signs in 2013 as the Lunar Node moved through Water-sign Scorpio. However, that year saw near spectacular growth across all major indices. By then the Node was half-way through the upswing of its cycle: the combined forces resulting in a surge or increase in share values.

It thus appears that the combination of Mercury retrograde and Lunar Node in the same element coincides with strong financial tides. Readers might like to note a repeat of these conditions when Mercury retrogrades in Water signs from late 2019 and throughout 2020, as the Lunar Node is in Cancer (a Water sign) and in the second (declining) half of the McWhirter Lunar cycle. The next time that Mercury is retrograde in a Water sign as the Node makes passage through a Water sign—when prices should increase—is in August 2032, when a quick swell should see prices quickly rise.

Though Mercury retrograde periods often coincide with negative trading conditions (which are also promising buying conditions), the sectors most likely to be affected vary hugely.

In 2001, the dot-com crash, though affecting many indices, had greatest impact on the new and apparently exciting technology industries developing at the turn of the millennium. While the most dramatic falls in this sector were in 2000 when emphasis was on the Water element, they continued through 2001 and 2002 as the Mercury retrogrades and lunar Node moved to Air signs: by which time another market sector was affected.

Even before the horrendous 9/11 attack, the Mercury Air retrograde periods had proved volatile—with the S&P index falling as Mercury retrograded through both Gemini and Aquarius. As we know, air- and travel-related stocks plunged. It could be these that are caught in the slip stream of financial dramas in the second quarter of 2021, when once again there is emphasis on the element of Air.

It is worth mentioning that the length of Mercury's retrograde periods vary according to how close that planet is to the Sun. Mercury's retrograde moves through the Fire signs are relatively short. The longest period is as it moves through Water signs. Note too that the sequence of Mercury retrogrades is in reverse order to that of the usual movement through the signs of the zodiac. The Sun moves from Fire, to Earth, to Air, and then to Water signs. Mercury retrogrades do the opposite. A full list of Mercury direct and retrograde dates including degrees and signs is given in Appendix 5.

Since the Millennium, Mercury has retrograded in Fire signs in 2004–2005, throughout 2011, and 2017–2018. The 2004–2005 retrogrades coincided with the Lunar Node moving through Aries, and as the McWhirter cycle indicated probable equity price rises. The 2017–2018 retrogrades coincided with the Lunar Node at the apparent "top" of this cycle in Leo. The next retrogrades will take place as the Lunar Node travels through on the way to the bottom of this cycle. These periods may well offer buying opportunities but will surely be disquieting for those already invested and who fear a falling market.

As you might imagine, the sector associated with Fire signs is the energy sector. In each of the years listed, it is this sector that has been particularly volatile. From the fourth quarter of 2023 and through the first two quarters of 2024—as Mercury is retrograde in a Fire sign and as the Node moves through Fire-sign Aries (the downside of the cycle)—this sector should experience greatest decline. It is during this period that oil prices should be at a low.

The pattern of retrograde Mercury in Earth signs is just as interesting and informative when combined with this Lunar Node position by sign. Note first that moving backwards through the zodiac (as the Node moves) between Leo (the top of the cycle) and Aquarius (the bottom), the only Earth sign is Taurus— already marked as a sign associated with banking and with material values. We should expect that when retrograde Mercury in Taurus coincides with the Lunar Node in Taurus, commodity prices will be affected (to the down side) and that banking stock might similarly fall.

In the fourth quarter of 2003, Mercury was retrograde in Earth sign Capricorn as the Node moved through Taurus. Not only did the gold index rise, but indices too rose through these weeks. We might then deduce that the "Taurus" effect worked and that the nodes position in this sign acted as a contrary force. This is important to note as the Node will pass through this sign again between December 2021 and July 2023. From December 2022 and through 2023, Mercury's retrograde periods are in either Capricorn or Taurus. It may be that through these weeks, we see a rise in the gold index and in share prices as we did in 2003.

All data should help us predict when "rats" and "disease" are most likely to appear but also indicates a period ahead when the trend could be reversed and we might make gain.

Problems and Personal Finance

So far we have only considered Mercury's retrograde periods. There is little doubt that these are important: the moment irritations may threaten our provisions unless they are dealt with quickly. For example, you may find at such times that minor difficulties give rise to increased costs (repairs), or find yourself working for less or even no pay.

At a personal level it is useful to think back to years when you made financial progress—and years when you did not. You may discover a pattern. In the case of "bad" years when, at the financial level you experienced severe challenges, in what type of sign did Mercury retrograde? Was it Fire, Earth, Air, or Water?

The degrees covered during Mercury's retrograde passage should be carefully noted. Occasionally Mercury will move back into a sign of a different element: for example making its first station at, e.g., 14 degrees of Aries (a Fire Sign) and retrograding back into Pisces (a Water sign). This type of retrograde period often brings chaos—and at many levels. That chaos can easily impinge on budgets resulting in these times being super-expensive for some. An excellent example of this happened with a client who put out a marketing brochure just as Mercury began to turn retrograde. As Mercury moved back into the earlier sign, the demand for these catalogues increased. The eventual cost of this exercise far exceeded that which had been anticipated. Further, though demand for the catalogue was high, this was not reflected in later sales.

Mercury never travels far from the Sun (as viewed from Earth). In fact, it can only venture at most 28 degrees away. That means though that the position of Mercury in your chart is not necessarily in the same sign as your Sun. You may be born with the Sun in Libra but Mercury could be in that sign or in either of the neighboring signs: Virgo or Scorpio.

If you have this information, then as you explore your financial history, you may find that tricky years coincide with years when your natal Mercury (after all the planet associated with commerce) was in incompatible elements with the retrograde Mercury periods. For example, if you have a natal Fire Mercury, and Mercury retrogrades in Water, you may feel that cold water is thrown on your financial position.

By contrast, a Fire Mercury (Aries, Leo or Sagittarius) might respond well to those years when Mercury retrogrades in an Air sign. After all, Air loves playing with Fire and can whip up a red hot heat.

Even without this information, and using only the position of the Sun, we can still determine years when "pests" are likely to appear in your financial cabin. Prominent amongst these are likely to be years when Mercury retrogrades in the element OPPOSITE the solar position.

My brother was born with both the Sun and Mercury in the Water sign of Pisces. During his working years he experienced two years of extreme financial difficulty. The first was in 1976 and the second in 2009. The intensity of the financial distress in 1976 was experienced as Mercury moved through Virgo—the sign opposite Pisces. Two other tricky years were negotiated—though these did not take him and his business quite "to the brink." These were years in which Mercury retrograded in Pisces. The balancing "champagne" years coincided with Mercury retrogrades in Fire signs.

In my own chart, financial pressures have again been most acute as Mercury's retrogrades moved through Aries (opposing my natal Sun and Mercury) and, for a few months, as Mercury retrograded in Libra. (For astrologers, please note that on neither of these occasions did Mercury station exactly on either my Sun or Mercury).

You can see this within organizations too. Recently, the company, Toys"R"Us collapsed. At its British incorporation on April 16, 1984, the Sun was in Aries and Mercury in Taurus. The company went into court-supervised administration in 2018 as Mercury retrograded in Aries.

Another tale: a Libra client invested in a buy-to-let property in 2014 (Mercury retrograding in Air signs). The income covered both the mortgage and a small income stream, and there were few difficulties. She decided to sell the property during a year when Mercury retrograded in Earth signs. Agents declared that the property would be easy to sell but failed to find buyers. They fared no better as the retrograde moved into Fire signs. Indeed, at this point they suggested that she lower the price. Though there were many other factors to be considered, it has become clear that divesting this property is unlikely before Mercury retrogrades are again in Air signs (2020–2021).

Another client, a Pisces (though Mercury was in Aries), experienced severe financial tension throughout 2013 and 2014. Pressure was acute through Mercury's retrograde period in 2013. Unable to find a solution, matters deteriorated further in 2014 as Mercury retrograded again in Pisces, though a satisfactory resolution was found as the retrograde moved into an Air sign that summer.

One of my most interesting cases though concerns someone born with both the Sun and Mercury in Sagittarius. The deals with which he is involved are always global and involve, to me, fantastic figures. He lives simply and has no real interest in the wealth he creates and generates: for him, the focus is on his philanthropic activities (usually involving school building). He does, however, sail very close to the wind and, not so long ago, seemed to be on the point of destitution. Obviously there is far more to be considered than the simple Sun-Mercury position. Even so, it is fascinating to note that the most difficult period occurred in 2015 as Mercury retrograded in each of the Air signs. It was almost as though there was so much Air, that his Fire was almost blown out.

Not only were the remaining embers reignited, but, as the retrograde Mercury's progressed through the Fire signs in 2017, business picked up and took off—big-time. At the time of writing, and with another retrograde Mercury period due at the end of 2018, it seems clear that he will be one of the world's high financial flyers.

Trading with Mercury Retrograde

The short advice here is: Don't!—unless you are an experienced trader. It is only those able to combine technical analysis with understanding of Mercury's cycle who should be considered best placed to make gain through these often treacherous periods.

When Mercury is retrograde—in whatever sign—there is usually confusion and, importantly, changeability. Unless, like the winged-messenger, unless you are quick on your feet, it is wise not to trade. Prices are unlikely to be stable, misinformation abound, and the stock price move contrarily. Such periods are better used for studying financial papers, exploring the background of companies, and then—having carried out this risk assessment— making purchase after Mercury returns to the position held at the start of its retrograde phase.

Note that this is not the same as Mercury's direct station. To be clear: Mercury turns retrograde and then, a couple of weeks later appears (as viewed from Earth) to stand still once more (the direct station). It is not until it returns to the retrograde degree, when it completes its apparent loop in the sky, that the "danger" period can be said to have concluded.

Inferior and Superior Conjunctions

Within Mercury retrograde periods, there are special dates when the Sun and Mercury are exactly aligned. The Superior conjunction occurs when—if we could see through the Sun—it would appear that the Sun and Mercury were in exact alignment. An inferior conjunction occurs when the Sun is between the Earth and Mercury. The superior conjunction is important and worth marking in your trading diary. It usually marks a day of increased volume of trade. It rarely marks a turning point but is a day of unusually high activity.

The ancients described both conjunctions as "combust"

since Mercury appeared to be "burned up" by the Sun. In fact, though the day of the exact conjunction has been known to bring major confusion, it's as true to say that the days on either side of this—perhaps as many as five—result in crazed activity both in the marketplace and elsewhere. These dates are perhaps better used for contemplation—and certainly not for trading, unless you have considerable expertise.

It is worth mentioning that when a Sun-Mercury conjunction occurs in the signs of either Cancer or Virgo, there is often a change in the direction of wheat and corn prices. These conjunctions will, of course, take place during the summer months. At the Cancer conjunction, farmers gain some idea of the potential harvest. At the Virgo conjunction, they have an even better idea of the size and quality of the crop. This information results in a strong market move. This isn't necessarily an indicator of pending problems: either date could mark recovery.

Company fortunes are often affected (infected occasionally!) by Mercury retrograde periods. Yet these have to be set against the entire and usually complex cosmic background surrounding the company's first trade. Attention should be given to the position of Mercury in that chart. Readers may be surprised to learn that many longstanding and successful companies were launched when Mercury was retrograde, making it clear that Mercury's retrograde status is not necessarily a "bad" thing. That does not mean that Mercury's status is irrelevant. Many techniques are used to determine a company's likely good fortune—or the opposite. Astro-traders studying the fortunes of a company will also take into account market reaction around earlier Mercury retrograde and direct dates—and Sun-Mercury conjunctions—and factor this information into their forecasting.

For example, General Electric (GE) was trading at $42 per share on October 5, 2007, but just $7 in March 2009 at the low of the global financial crisis. Recall that the Lunar Node was moving through Aquarius—the low of the business cycle—and that the astro-trader would not have been looking for sharp rises in price through this period, but more likely for falls.

GE was certainly experiencing an "infection" or fever at the

March low. What is interesting is that the price reached not quite $13.58 (almost double its low) at the first Mercury retrograde station following the low. Sharpest movements came on the day of the inferior conjunction and at the direct station. The next Mercury retrograde saw the price break through a trend line. The share price then rose into the inferior conjunction ($18) before falling until the Superior conjunction on November 4, 2009 ($14).

Of course it is true that many other companies suffered dramatic losses during this same period and that like GE, they have yet to recover that earlier value. Yet there is a difference between GE share price movement—and its reaction to Mercury retrogrades—and the share price of other businesses.

To understand this we need to know more about Mercury's position when GE was first traded—just as an astrologer would do with your own chart when assessing your "commercial sense." As you will see in the example below, it is not just Mercury's zodiacal position that is taken into account but the interconnectedness with other planets too.

The chart for first trade is the best indicator as to vulnerability to commercial infection. The most recent first trade data for General Electric is for May 27, 1926 (although GE was also traded from June 23, 1892). Tracking today's share price movement is best done from the most recent IPO.

In this (1926) chart, Mercury is situated in a late degree of Taurus and a full 9 degrees from the Sun position. It is by no means "combust," nor is that planet retrograde. It does however oppose Saturn, and is at right angles to both Jupiter and Neptune which are in opposition to one another. We know from GE's longevity that this is not a "weak" chart but it does suggest that when "infected" it will take a long time (links to Saturn and Neptune) to recover. A planetary picture of Mercury with Jupiter, Saturn, and Neptune conjures images of chronic infection or pneumonia rather than simple common cold, and an infection that might linger.

General Electric's trend in share price warrants a close look at long-term cycles (the Lunar Node being the most dominant) before assessing Mercury's potential impact. Since 2009, GE's share price has peaked again at approximately $14: coinciding with Uranus' conjunction with Venus in the 1926 chart. The price has since fallen to a low of $11, presumably affected by Uranus' transit over Chiron in May 2018.

If we held shares in this company, we would surely wonder just how low the price might fall, and if, indeed, we should hold on in the hope of a price rise. Before coming to a decision, we would take many factors into consideration (not least technical analysis), but might wonder if Mercury's retrograde and direct stations would give buy or sell signals. In the first trade chart, Mercury was in Earth sign Taurus.

We know that Mercury retrograded in Earth signs in 2010 and again in 2016 and the first retrograde of 2017. Research reveals that the retrograde periods (up to and including Mercury's return to the retrograde degree) were particularly volatile. Through 2010, the price moved between $14 and $19—a wide range. The Earth retrograde periods of 2016–2017 saw a similar range: from $33 at the start to $28. The drop in value continued, and was particularly marked later in 2017 as Mercury moved through Scorpio and opposed its First Trade position.

In 2022, Mercury will once again be retrograde in earth signs. Interesting—a least as far as GE is concerned—its direct station in May of that year is within a degree of its natal position and may well mark a period of marked price moves.

In Conclusion

What we have discovered in this chapter is firstly that it's important to acknowledge vulnerability to commercial pestilence and yes, potential devastation. Assuming though that we are not affected by a pandemic, and that our focus is on short periods when we need to be on commercial guard, we have learned that with even just a little knowledge of Mercury's cosmic rhythm we can do much to protect ourselves from financial harm.

CHAPTER 4

Points of Reference

We need fixed points of reference. Knowing when and where disaster might strike is essential. As does the pilot of any ship, we need to set our course and know where the lighthouses are along the way. These alert us to dangers. The arrangement of the planets and eclipse paths provides us with that information. With understanding of our cosmic habitat—where we have come from and where we are within key planetary cycles—we are in good position to identify potential financial rocks and tsunamis.

We first take into account the various icebergs that we will encounter in the challenging decade from 2020 to 2030 which can be threatening to our financial stability. A few of these "icebergs" look huge—yet they may be masked by clouds, and many people will be hopelessly unaware of the danger until it is too late to take evasive action.

It is imperative, therefore, that we are alert to potential dangers in the formidable cosmic seas ahead. We need to be as familiar as possible with these hidden threats. Keep in mind your twin destinations: survival and long-term security.

2020

The extraordinary planetary alignments in 2020, and mentioned in the opening chapter, are formidable—not just because of the number of planets that will group on one side of the Sun—but because that concentration of energy is in one sign of the zodiac, Capricorn: the sign associated with banking and corporate structures. Recall that it was Pluto's entry into this sign in 2008 that coincided with various banking scandals. Many loans were described as "toxic"—a keyword connected to Pluto.

Although much work has been done to clean up the banking system and to overcome the very real difficulties that defaults would have posed, debts have yet to be cleared. Few of those who were at the helm during those turbulent years have been held to account. Some are still in positions of financial authority. There is certainly little reassuring evidence to indicate that all problems have been overcome, that there is a revised outlook, that the system has been restructured and is safe, or that a repeat cannot occur.

From the cosmic perspective, there is much to suggest that calamity lies in wait. The fact that three of the slower moving planets change signs within the space of just a few years (2023–2025) is indicative of tidal waves that could yet engulf many nations.

Again, debts have not been reduced. Though sub-prime mortgages are no longer the problem, there is evidence of other loans being made available in a similar fashion (e.g., for car purchases) which almost certainly will not be paid off. How these were "bank-rolled" is questionable. Governments may yet be held to account for not putting more stringent lending criteria in place. The scale of disaster may be different to that of 2007–2008, but until Pluto leaves Capricorn (2024), the possibility of another and yet greater global financial crisis than the last should not be discounted.

The bond market warrants particular attention. From the planetary picture perspective there is much to suggest that a bubble is growing and that it will burst before Pluto leaves Capricorn. Note that in recent years Neptune has been moving through Pisces. It is quite possible that many have been so happy to watch the bubble grow, that they have not thought through the consequences of its eventual—and inevitable—collapse. The threat might not be immediately obvious. Indeed, the bursting of this bubble, though it might begin in 2020 could be protracted and not conclude until 2022—at least according to planetary cycles.

Indeed, planetary alignments prior to December 2020 imply that some bonds will be thought to offer safe haven. Even so, for the watchful (those using planetary cycles), there should be signs that the fundamental structure of many of these is unsafe and that it is only a matter of time before they collapse.

A quick review of recent times is helpful:

In December 2017, and only two days before the December solstice, Saturn entered Capricorn to join Pluto in that sign. Venus moved into Capricorn four days later. Though this is not the heavy concentration of Capricorn energy expected in January 2020—when no fewer than six planets will be grouped in this area of the zodiac—the planetary picture of December 2017 offered a hint of what is to come.

It should not surprise us that as Saturn moved into Capricorn, indices which had been climbing, suffered setback. European stock markets were most negatively impacted following news of the Catalan referendum that threatened breakaway from Spain. The FTSE (UK exchange) fell from a record high and Spain's IBEX futures lost over one percent value in the course of the day.

While those markets recovered fairly quickly, we should nevertheless take note of the negative mood. Negativity is a direct result of fearfulness and lack of confidence. While these markets did indeed recover as the Sun and Venus (much faster moving than Saturn and Pluto) moved out of Capricorn, this grouping left its mark. There is still threat of repeat.

Until Uranus' discovery in 1781, Saturn's orbit was the longest within the known solar system. Saturn is often thought of as a patroller, old father time, or boundary master. When this planet is at work, then there is a demand to meet and preferably exceed expectations. Tests and inspections must be passed and work shown to have been done to the highest standard. If work hasn't been carried out or is deemed inadequate, then Saturn demands retesting.

Once there is an even larger grouping of planets in Capricorn in December 2019, we should expect fear to take hold and last longer. We should also anticipate impacts across global markets, as by then the Lunar Node will be in the downward half of its cycle. If history does repeat, this coincides with loss of market confidence and a fall in share prices.

To repeat: Capricorn is the sign associated with banking. A strong possibility is that from mid-2019, banks will apply ever tighter criteria to their loan offerings. Interest rates (savings and loans) will surely rise. While savers will be understandably delighted to see raised income, those seeking financial support for businesses experiencing cash flow difficulties will be far less so. Their position might even become untenable. So that by the solar eclipse in mid-2019, there will be signs of an increase in the number of applications for insolvency, Chapter 11 or bankruptcy.

Strengthening this possibility is Jupiter's passage through Capricorn in 2019–2020. This planet has a reputation for excess: whether to the negative or positive. We might expect aggressive marketing of bonds, even while many of those in charge are aware that their value cannot be guaranteed

Again, this transit bodes well for savers, but is a probable indicator of rising costs for those seeking funding. The gulf between the haves and have-nots will surely widen.

It is interesting that prior to the forming of this group of planets in Capricorn, and perhaps masking "ice-rocky masses" or "icebergs" from view, are the recent ingresses of both Uranus and Chiron in 2018–2019. The combination of these planetary energies provides what might be described as an electronic fog that can only be navigated by those with the best satellite guidance systems.

Recall that when the slower-moving bodies of the cosmic system change signs, there tends to be at least a ripple if not a crisis in financial markets. It is unusual for Uranus and Chiron to make ingress within the same twelve month period: not rare, but certainly unusual. In the recent past they each made ingress in 1995 and, before that, in 1988.

In 1995, President Clinton invoked emergency powers to extend a $20 billion loan to help Mexico avert financial crash. This came to be known as the "Tequila Crash." In 1988, Norway experienced a banking crisis from which, as with the Mexico crisis, it took some years to recover—and whose financial ripples were felt far from Norway's shores. The Norwegian crisis was the first major banking crisis in Europe since World War II. Following deregulation, Norwegian banks engaged in what would later be termed "risky credit operations." So began a lending boom halted in 1985 when oil prices fell significantly—eventually resulting in the devaluation of the Krone (Norwegian currency).

What we can recognize is that negotiating the two very different currents created by ingresses of both the planet Uranus and planetoid Chiron within a short period has, in the past, resulted in potentially contagious financial drama. Whether it is Brexit or another event, the banking community and governments should be on red alert for a major crisis before the end of 2019 as in that year Uranus makes Taurus ingress while Chiron moves to Aries.

The year 2019 is also exactly ninety years from the Wall Street Crash. The number of years is interesting in that it represents a quarter of a circle. It is worth investigating units of ninety years backwards from 1929 to see if there was any corresponding developments in global finances in those years. If we turn the wheel a whole cycle (360 degrees) from 1929, with each degree representing a year, we arrive at 1659. There is evidence of the first hand-written check being written that year. It is entirely possible that 2019 will mark the last example of this form of financial transaction—which, in recent years, has been used with decreasing frequency as the number of on-line transactions has soared.

The year 1749 (270 years back from 1929) and 1839 (180 years) provide further examples of major events affecting commercial transaction. The Royal Bank of Scotland was formed in 1749, while in 1839 Hambros and London and County banks were incorporated. Both institutions and the financial transactions and systems that they put in place have had huge effect in the last few hundred years, though we may all recognize that many of these systems are now at their "sell-by" date and that new systems are now needed.

From this information we might reasonably conclude that 2019 will mark the close of one phase of financial transacting while simultaneously marking the initial stages of new ways of working. These new ways of working must obviously incorporate accelerated developments in digital banking and crypto-currency management. For many people—and especially those who consider themselves to be technophobes, but who are forced to move to digital accounting to manage their money—this will likely present a financial iceberg.

2019

Arguably the dominant feature of 2019 will be the Solar Minimum. Though our Sun appears to have a regular sunspot rhythm, it is not exact and we cannot be sure that the number of sunspots will increase in the following minima as has happened during previous cycles. Indeed, as explained in the opening chapter, there is concern that there will be few if any sunspots during the whole of the next cycle (Sunspot Cycle 25.)*

What we can say with some confidence is that in the coming cycle, the number of sunspots is likely to be very low and, if the past repeats, that this will coincide with diminishing activity across all markets. Add to this, the expected business downturn as signalled by the Nodal cycle and we could witness very sharp falls indeed.

In 2019, weather extremes will be more the norm than the exception. By this time several planets—including Jupiter, the largest of the known planets—will be grouped on one side of the Sun. This should have significant effect on solar behavior. Either coronal mass ejection or strong solar winds may cause the malfunction of some satellite systems. Food distribution services would thus be adversely affected, making it imperative that local networks are in good order. Compensating for major outages may not be possible.

In February 2019, Chiron makes its final crossing into Aries. Less than a month later, Uranus arrives in Taurus. Both Chiron and Uranus will have spent some months in these signs during 2018 but then retrograded back before reaching these, the last and final ingresses into these signs for many years. Both ingresses bring the possibility of major financial incident. And yes, it is reasonable to expect that those born under these sun-signs will feel the immediate effect. Those born with the Sun in Aries may

---

* For the last few hundred years, sunspot cycles have been numbered (from minimum through maximum sunspot number and back to minimum). We are presently in the concluding phase of Sunspot Cycle 24 with Cycle 25 likely to begin around 2020.)

have reason to wonder if financially they are over-stretched and so need to rein in activity, while those born under Taurus will feel rising desire to do their own thing: possibly resulting in starting their own business.

During Chiron's brief sojourn into Aries in 2018, which coincided with Uranus' venture into the early degrees of Taurus, trade muscles were flexed as tariffs were announced. The full implementation of these is scheduled for 2019 and will have a huge effect on world economies.

Though Chiron has gained a reputation as "the wounded warrior," the position of that planetoid within a chart might also be described as the "maverick point." Doing things differently and problem-solving with a twist seem to be part of Chiron's hallmark. Aries is the "Tarzan" of the zodiac, moving with confidence and at speed. With regard to money as opposed to trade, we might reasonably expect that cash will do the same as Chiron arrives in this sector of the zodiac. The speedy transfer of money from one place to another—perhaps without recourse to a clearing house—is a strong possibility. At the time of writing, over 2000 crypto-currencies are in existence. By 2020 many more will have been launched but quickly died. It may not be possible to avoid their use, but choosing which one (or more than one) in which to handle day to day transactions will not be easy.

Aries is generally not noted for good risk management. Many people (not only those born with the Sun in this sign) may find that they are adversely affected by these tantalizing swift transactions, but which offer little by way of security.

Uranus brings shocks and surprises: words not usually associated with Taurus, whose key words include: "plodding," "stable," and "steady of purpose." The turbulence that coincides with Uranus' Taurus ingress might well result in terror in the financial industries as though a bull were on the loose in a china shop. Only those ornaments that are well locked up may be safe from this potential stampede. It is entirely possible that there will be a run on more than one bank as fears about security grow.

Uranus has visited this area of the zodiac before: between 1934 and 1942. While history has a tendency to repeat, it is usually as variations on a theme since the cosmos only replicates exact planetary positions approximately every 26,000 years. There were many reasons for the failures of over 9,000 banks during the 1930s. A common cosmic thread though is that these occurred post a square aspect between Uranus and Pluto, and as Uranus moved through Taurus. Uranus and Pluto completed a similar square aspect in 2015. Everyone then should be alert to the possibility of repetition of those earlier times. Bank failures may well begin in 2019 with the number of those failing accelerating as the decade draws to a close.

2020 Reference Points

In 2020 the Moon will come closer to Earth than it has been for over a decade. The combination of this special lunar perigee with solar minima will doubtless be a major factor in disturbed weather conditions—quite probably bringing drought to the southern hemisphere especially. Though this area is already experiencing extreme conditions, 2020 could see these worsen considerably. With that comes the high probability of increased food prices as crops become scarce.

It is not just lunar perigee that will doubtless attract the attention of sky-watchers. They will observe, even with the naked eye, Jupiter and Saturn moving ever closer to one another throughout the year until their conjunction—which coincides with the December solstice.

Before that date, we are, in effect, witnessing the close of the last cycle which began in May 2000. The 2020 cycle began with Jupiter and Saturn in Taurus an Earth sign, while the next is in Gemini an Air sign. The move from tangible and hard currency (Earth) to less tangible Air-type currencies is signaled. By the end of 2020, digital currencies are likely to be the norm: a move that will doubtless be deeply concerning to older generations who may be easy prey to those more familiar with password-protected accounts. Care will need to be taken to protect those born as Pluto moved through Cancer (pre-1939) who may be particularly vulnerable.

2019 concludes with a solar eclipse on December 26, and the anniversary of the Boxing Day tsunami. Though it is to be hoped that there no repeat of this natural and awful disaster, it is not uncommon for there to be natural disasters between a solar and lunar eclipse.

Worryingly, the chart for the lunar eclipse on January 10, 2020 has the Moon in Cancer, opposing an awesome stellium (grouping) of planets, together with the Sun in Capricorn. The subsequent pull of the planets—including Earth—on the Sun may well coincide with severe solar disturbance. It is not hard to imagine "the lights going out."

Prior to January 2020, we should all take what steps we can to insure that we could cope in the event of loss of power. It would surely also be wise to have debt contained or at least manageable by the start of this potentially financially tumultuous year.

Capricorn is associated with prudence and with austerity. In 2020 we should expect revaluations in property markets. Banks may be unable or unwilling to lend. The resulting stalemate could see prices falling and property market stagnation.

It is fascinating to note that both solstice points—zero degrees of cardinal signs—in 2020 are marked by two key celestial events: June 21 by an eclipse whose path cuts from Zaire, through Saudi Arabia, India, and southern China; and the December solstice with the very special Jupiter-Saturn conjunction named the Grand Mutation. This conjunction is the first of a series to last for 240 years.

What seems clear is that in 2020, the whole world will be faced with financial rocks and that steering ships around these will be super-challenging. There is no generation alive today that has coped with anything remotely similar. Given that we often learn by experience, the lack of earlier challenge will require that we each access levels of courage and bravery as we face potential adversity. Just as ships of old encountered cross-currents and tempestuous seas as they rounded the Capes of Good Hope and Horn, in 2020 globally we are faced with comparable challenges. Avoiding being shipwrecked will require that our provisions are held in the strongest hull possible.

Countries

Whichever timed chart is used for the United States of America, the date of the signing of its Constitution is agreed as July 4, 1781. China's most recent chart is based on October 1, while Australia, Great Britain and many others have charts based on January 1. These charts—all with the Sun at virtual right angle to another—will all be affected by the arrangement of the planets in 2020.

The USA will likely be particularly affected. Its Sun position is at 13 degrees of Cancer: the exact degree of the Full Moon on July 5, 2020. The chart for this event should be viewed as a potential financial tsunami event that brings particular pressure on the US dollar. Mercury will be retrograde as the Sun conjoins Vesta: the asteroid associated with foreign exchange trading. It may be that the US dollar comes under considerable pressure if not at the date exactly, then between the Full Moon on July 5 and the New Moon which follows two weeks later.

In the New Moon chart of July 19, Saturn opposes the Moon exactly and could see not just the US dollar under pressure, but also sterling and perhaps various other currencies. Since this event coincides with the South Lunar Node aligning with the Galactic Center, it is not hard to imagine collapse in many prices: notably property, but affecting all asset classes.

It is a curious fact that seven hundred years ago, the Battle of Crecy, whose outcome shaped the history of England and France for many centuries, took place as Jupiter was at zero degrees of one of the Cardinal signs. There are numerous other instances suggesting that the course of history is much altered by events taking place at these points. Given that the June 21 solar eclipse accents another of these cardinal degrees, it is likely that key events will bring similarly lasting consequences.

Having identified the major rocks of 2020 and determined the likelihood of buoys ahead, we can use our long-range radar to identify another period of significant change of financial current requiring us to alter course and to "man the decks."

2021–2024

As you might imagine, whenever the sign of Pisces is accented by the presence of slow-moving planets, waves are higher than usual—even as they are seductive. Since 2013, Neptune has been traveling through that sign: an area of the zodiac in which it is said to work well. The accompanying waves have at times been surf-friendly, luring the unwary onto rocks. Many traders have enjoyed the ups and downs of recent times. Imagine if you will, the impact of Jupiter joining Neptune in Pisces in 2021. Jupiter last visited this sign in 2010 when stocks, having hit a major low in 2009, made fast recovery. The ride was wonderful for those who were not risk averse and who climbed back in to the markets despite the debacle of the previous few years.

The swell and waves may not be quite as seductive in 2021, since the Lunar Node will be moving to the low in the business cycle. Rather we might expect that these large waves will threaten to damage provisions (savings and pensions especially). Unable to reach port with ease, we will need to have confidence in the strength of our ship's hull to cope with large water swells. Meetings with financial advisors—preferably in 2020 before these expected rough cosmic seas are to be recommended. It may be advisable to move some funds to guaranteed or low-risk areas.

In February 2021, Saturn and Uranus reach their last quarter phase. It is worth remembering that the development of crypto-currencies has developed in tandem with the unfolding of this cycle. The first rocks to appear in 2021 will likely alert us to the dangers of such currencies, perhaps propelling us back to the apparent safety of hard currencies. The February "lighthouse" should be seen as the first of a series of three: the next appearing in June 2021, and the last—which warns not just of rocks but of potential disease—in December of that year.

Though it might seem strange to write about the chart of a currency, there is a recognized, working chart for the US dollar: April 2, 1792, Philadelphia—exact time unknown. To check whether or not a chart "works" it is necessary to look back to see what effect, if any, planetary movements have had on this chart.

Having satisfied ourselves that there has been correlation, we can then make forecasts.

It is fascinating to note—an extraordinary piece of cosmic coincidence or poetry—that Neptune opposes the exact position of Mars in this chart in February 2021. This implies a weakening in dollar strength. This will not be the first time that Neptune has opposed the Mars of this chart: it happened through 1856 and 1857 which was an interesting period for that currency.

Until 1857, foreign coins, including the Spanish dollar were accepted as legal tender. The weight of silver in US silver coins had been reduced a few years earlier, which had effectively placed the nation on the gold standard. While there cannot be an exact replication, we can reasonably assume that there will once again be a change in the way in which that currency operates: perhaps allowing the US dollar to lose value while also making room for one or more crypto-currencies to gain prominence. Three days after this aspect is exact, Jupiter opposes Uranus in this same chart, supporting the idea of breakthrough that comes through the use of developing technologies.

Study of the Saturn-Uranus cycle reveals that for at least the last few hundred years, as each exact aspect formed, financial obstacles appeared. To be clear: those "exact aspects" do not have to be the conjunction, opposition or even the first or last quarter phase. These two planets are always in relationship to one another. Even when they are a fifth, seventh, eleventh, or even seventeenth of a cycle apart from one another (within a half-degree), a financial obstacle appears.

Present day United States of America came into being when these two planets were a third of a cycle apart. This goes some way toward explaining why financial icebergs have appeared in the USA when the two planets were once again in aspect to one another: it is as though the nation is primed and ready for financial development at each phase of this cycle. Indeed, in one version of the USA chart, Saturn is positioned in the "financial risk and speculation" area. It was perhaps hoped that solid legislation would keep any rogue elements in check and ensure that any risks were adequately assessed. History however shows that any cautious assessment is thrown to the winds when Uranus arrives: most times leading to financial debacle.

That a key aspects between these two planets in February 2021 coincides with Chiron's station at a recognized critical degree of the zodiac underlines the potential for catastrophe: possibly viral and with global consequences. This could be technical, affecting digital currencies but might also be an indicator of wide spread infection, warranting control of the movement of people as opposed to financial transactions: even though the economic impact of restricted movement would surely be considerable.

Assuming successful negotiation of 2021, the year 2022 offers a calmer sea. Though it is true that the year is unlikely to pass without financial incident, it does not appear to offer the threatening conditions of 2021. Indeed, by November 2022, some may feel that the worst is behind them. This conclusion would not be wise. As of the first of that month Mars turns retrograde. Think of this as the sea pulling back before delivering a tsunami.

March 2023 should be red-ringed in every trader's diary. In the space of a month, Jupiter, Saturn, and Pluto all change signs (as viewed from Earth). We know that a single ingress brings a ripple. The combined force of three such events—including Pluto's move into Aquarius, might even bring panic. True, it is possible that this period will see great political and social upheaval for the greater good. Yet drama in the financial markets will likely be inconvenient if not disastrous. The weeks between the solar eclipse on April 20 and the accompanying lunar eclipse two weeks later may be particularly difficult to negotiate.

It is most interesting that on May 16, 2023 Jupiter enters Taurus. Uranus made similar ingress on May 15, 2018. These dates are very close indeed to the birthdate of the New York Stock Exchange (May 17) and are exactly six months from the birthdate of the Johannesburg exchange. The fact that major cosmic events coincide with this anniversary indicates firstly that the ensuing twelve months will see marked difference in the pulse of trading, and also that the sectors demanding the most attention—and showing greatest movement—will differ greatly from those of the preceding year.

Jupiter's arrival in any sign usually heralds expansion in commercial activities associated with that sign (see last chapter for more information). That this particular transit coincides with both Uranus and the Lunar Node moving through that sign (and on its downward descent) suggests that expansion will be limited to those companies with the most secure asset base. The probability under these conditions is that trade will be limited to those using hard cash (the emphasis on Earth signs) given that the digital money supply may be compromised and recovering from difficulties at the start of the year.

Recall that Pluto is just the first of the slower moving planets to be changing signs in the mid 2020s. As is normal, and as viewed from Earth, owing to a retrograde period, that planet slips back into Capricorn before making full ingress in 2024. The second half of 2023 provides a hint of the seas to come, their revised depth (Pluto is God of the Underworld), and alerts us to the potential dangers of having insufficient provisions for the next stage of our financial journey.

Those who have not given thought as to provisions will need to find port and make adjustment. The realization that certain industries are changing beyond recognition, that they have too much investment in sectors that are losing value, will likely give way to panic—leading to yet poorer decision making.

It will surely be necessary during 2024, as Pluto moves back and forth over the Capricorn-Aquarius border, to have life rafts at the ready for the great waves building. The situation by then should be obvious to all. Not setting sail won't be an option. The best that those ill-equipped can hope to do is to be part of a flotilla of small rafts where all help and shelter one another. Even then, it may be difficult to avoid being displaced or struck by greater ships.

Recession

There are several cosmic clues suggesting that the period 2023–2028 will be financially challenging. You may know that there is a definite cycle to recessions: linking the lunar nodal cycle and

Jupiter's transits through the twelve signs. No two recessions are driven by the same causes and, as might be expected, each has a slightly altered planetary picture to an earlier one. What is clear is that there is a cosmic pattern or rhythm to these events. This pattern has operated now for two centuries. Of course there is no guarantee that humankind will march to this rhythm yet again: yet we must consider this possibility. If you know that a recession is coming, even if you can't avoid the full impact, you can take steps to secure assets, hopefully boost savings, and look for alternative ways to stay afloat.

If the past is indeed a reflection of the future, then the recession of 2025–2027 will surely affect all asset classes—including property and land prices. Those with mortgages taken out in earlier years could find this an exceedingly tough period as property prices fall and negative equity becomes the norm.

The negative effects of recession are easy to enumerate: lost jobs, lost income, bankruptcy, etc. Companies are forced to rethink their business model. Consider those companies formed at the end of the nineteenth century and still going strong, having survived the many recessions of the twentieth century and the global financial crisis of 2007. Some will surely survive the next financial crisis.

Though loss of employment is a debilitating experience, the past shows that there are people who negotiate the trauma, and eventually move from employment that may have been joyless and unrewarding into areas that allow them to explore and make the most of their natural talents. A recession can, and often does, mark a period of rebalancing. Yes, it is usually painful, but with foreknowledge, it can be prepared for. It should also be remembered that "nothing lasts forever," and that though a recession is an awful period, the gray skies do eventually lift.

As stated, all recessions are different. The recession of 2025–2028 will surely be like no other since it hits just as other major economic and social cycles get under way. These cycles, of varying length, are linked to the position of the outer planets: three of which will have made recent ingress by 2025. If one slow-moving planet brings financial turbulence, then three changing signs in a period of just a few years threatens calamity. Between 2023 and 2025 we should expect turbulent financial seas and the possibility of global recession.

You could think of it this way: Pluto affects the undercurrents which may shift before we realize that our engines are working harder, that we are using more fuel, that costs are rising, and that we're not making progress. Meanwhile, Neptune's sign change may lure us into thinking that there is a fast and easy current not far away. This can bring the potential for us to self-sabotage by not taking preventative action and tightening our financial belts, and possibly by luring us into making investments that we can't afford and which result in us breaking our masts. Uranus meanwhile, having moved into Air sign, Gemini, will no doubt bring cross winds that are sufficiently fierce that mending the mast is beyond our capabilities.

The concluding stages of Pluto's transit through Capricorn may well coincide with reappraisal of taxation and pension arrangements. During Neptune's passage through Pisces, exploitation of rules and regulations has been rampant. Few have been called to account. Yet that time is likely coming—once Jupiter, Saturn, and Pluto are in Capricorn. Satisfying as this may be to many, those taking over their roles, even if free from any guilt, may lack experience. Having these individuals as harbor masters or pilots could lead to more mishaps especially in 2025.

Just as the ingresses of Chiron and Uranus to Aries and Taurus respectively indicated change of currents in 2018, so too do those of Neptune and Pluto in 2024–2025. Steering through these waves will surely require particular skill, given that both planets are moving to areas of the zodiac not yet visited in our lifetimes—or indeed those of our parents or grandparents: we have no living relatives with whom we can discuss those periods.

We are reliant on historical documents that recorded any singular financial activity as Neptune moved from Pisces to Aries, and Pluto from Capricorn to Aquarius. Neptune last made the Pisces-Aries crossing in 1861, while Pluto last moved from Capricorn to Aquarius in 1777. In neither year was there either a financial panic or debacle. However, in the case of the former, repayment of debts incurred during the American Civil War was an issue, while a year after Pluto last arrived in Aquarius in 1777, the US Treasury was reorganized.

It is entirely possible, given war cycle analysis, that war debt will be a key issue in the mid 2020s and that the US Treasury amongst other institutions will require restructuring. Events related to debt repayment and to institutional reorganization may be linked. Certainly turbulence is to be expected. It is probable that the financial waves will be high; taxing the skills of even the most experienced of financial advisors. Indeed, tax itself will likely need to be rethought.

Though the planetary signature for this recession is clear, the fact that it coincides with one of the more extraordinary planetary alignments suggests that this could be a bleak period indeed.

Inflation is likely to rise after Neptune leaves Pisces. A review of each of Neptune's passages through the Fire signs of Aries, Leo, or Sagittarius has coincided with price rises. During those years when Jupiter joins Neptune in a Fire sign, inflation has been the norm. The most recent occasion was in 1971 when both planets moved through Sagittarius. They will again be in Fire signs (Jupiter in Sagittarius and Neptune in Aries) in 2030. This will surely put pressure on those with fixed pensions.

2025–2026

The position of the planets is calculated by astronomers and astrologers alike from the first degree of Aries: that point where the Sun's path crosses the Earth's equator as projected into space. Of course there is nothing actually "there" at this point. However, it does mark the first day of Spring (in the Northern hemisphere) and is often considered to be the "human race" point. (After all, this point in the sky would have no relevance whatsoever if you lived on Mars—or indeed, anywhere else in the solar system.)

It is, though, a primary reference point for those of us on Earth. First degree Aries is a powerful position—as are the other "reference points' ninety degrees from this point. These mark what are known as the Cardinal points of the zodiac (first degrees of Aries, Cancer, Libra, and Capricorn—each of which marks an equinox or solstice). There is much to support this argument. History records that the passage of one of the slow moving planets across any one of these Cardinal points has coincided with periods of eventfulness. It is worth noting that those born with the Sun at these degrees tend to stand out from the crowd.

Saturn passes the first degree of Aries roughly every three decades, and Neptune approximately every 164 years, with their orbits coinciding roughly every forty-five years. It is rare however for their "meeting" or conjunction to take place at exactly zero degrees Aries.

The history of the Saturn-Neptune cycle, both from the mathematical or cosmological perspective and as events unfold on Earth, is fascinating. First look closely at the accompanying diagram. This traces the various Saturn-Neptune conjunctions over thousands of years. A very definite picture or form emerges.

If we examine social history, we find that the alignment and subsequent phase relationship of the Saturn-Neptune cycle correlates neatly with developments in socialism. Politically there is an apparent "lurch to the left" at the start of this cycle, and a similar resurgence of interest in that type of politics at both the square and opposition phases of their cycle.

Both planets are said to be "cold" places. Few of us have difficulty in conjuring up pictures of the sea when thinking of Neptune. We naturally think expansiveness and large waves. By contrast, Saturn promotes thoughts of cold and definite shapes: mountains to be conquered. Putting the two together, it is natural to imagine an iceberg. The 2026 conjunction at the "human race" point suggests an iceberg to be faced by the entire human race: one that could have devastating effect on global finances.

A quick review of the three Saturn-Neptune conjunctions of the twentieth century confirms a pattern: The first conjunction in 1917 coincided with the Russian Revolution and overthrow of the Tsars: a major social and political upheaval. It has been said that this revolution opened a trapdoor to the future. Certainly it was one of the major events of the twentieth century, with a legacy

This flowery diagram is a plot of the daily longitude and relative speed of the planets Saturn and Neptune. As the planets speed up it is drawn farther from the center, forming petals that look remarkably similar to the petals of some flowers.

This image has been created with the Sirius 3.0 software, which is a very flexible and powerful astrology software available from Cosmic Patterns Software at www.AstroSoftware.com.

that is still felt today. Researchers are now studying the links between this revolution and the private financiers of the time.

As viewed from Earth, the conjunction occurred three times in 1953. This was a momentous year at many levels: the coronation of Queen Elizabeth II, several major scientific breakthroughs including Crick's discovery of DNA, and further social upheaval in

Russia and Eastern Germany. At the economic level, the London Debt Agreement of that year saw the abolition of all Germany's external debt.

Eastern Europe was again in the headlines at the next conjunction in 1989 with the Fall of the Berlin Wall and the subsequent reunification of Germany. In an extraordinary act, one deutschmark from the East was given the same value as one from the West. 1989 was also the year of the junk bond crisis.

Though some might argue that every year is eventful, it must surely be agreed that there is a common thread linking 1917 to 1953 and 1989. Each of these years brought financial drama the effects of which last to this day.

It is quite reasonable to expect that 2026 will be another year of profound change and that events in Eastern Europe will play a significant role again. That the February conjunction of 2026 occurs during the period forecast for global recession suggests that this could be a period of misery for many.

It would be quite wrong to dismiss the possibility of global war through this period. The US entered WW I in 1917, just as the conjunction began to take effect. By the end of that war, only eighteen months later, over four million US personnel were involved. Given that the 2026 conjunction is at the first degree of Aries—a sign noted for courage, bravery and action and ruled by Mars—it is not unreasonable to suggest that mobilization following conscription will be a feature of this period.

War may well have begun some years earlier and it is entirely possible that the Saturn-Neptune conjunction at 0° Aries will be an indicator of the growing number of people sacrificed in the pursuit of whatever aim.

As there are at least two solar eclipses, and sometimes as many as five in any given year, we will not consider all those taking place in the coming years, but will look closely at one: the solar eclipse of September 21, 2025. The planetary formation surrounding this event is particularly special as it comes within a day of an equinox and in a year when an outer planet, Neptune, changes signs. It is very likely indeed that the financial seas will be tumultuous around this date with real danger of investors being thrown overboard. Many may choose to be out of the market long before this date but ready to buy back in at a convenient low.

By 2026, Pluto will have moved from Capricorn to Aquarius. As we saw earlier, this ingress is likely to coincide with developments in global finances, and it is perhaps not too much to suggest that redistribution of wealth will be a key factor.

2027–2030

By the close of 2030, at least in terms of global finance, it will likely seem that we have done the equivalent of "round the Cape." The storms, cross-currents, poor weather and visibility should be behind us. Though we might then wonder what lies ahead, it should be clear even as early as the close of 2027, that the seas are calmer, that there are safe ports, and that we have weathered the worst.

Even so, it would be wise not to drop our guard and to be aware of two major cycle phases dominating this period. The first is one with which we are already familiar: a critical phase in the Saturn-Pluto cycle associated with austerity, pruning, restructuring, and making do with little. As always, this will surely be a struggle for those with little experience. Anyone of working or pensionable age will have experience of this though, and might even find that working with these cosmic winds not too difficult: they might even enjoy re-trimming their sails.

Considerably less pleasant will surely be the first quarter square between Chiron and Pluto. Recall that Chiron is the faster moving of these two orbiting bodies and that the first quarter demands review of decisions and actions taken at the start of this cycle: December 30th 1999. (You may recall all the angst about a possible millennium computer bug that might bring down all systems leading to food shortages, lack of bank notes, etc., etc.). Although not everyone bought into this premise, there was fear that planes would be grounded and that travel was inadvisable. Given that the conjunction took place in the travel-related sign of Sagittarius, this was understandable, even if those fears were unfounded.

While it seems unlikely that a similar event will take place in the coming years, we should not rule out the possibility. We should also note that this first quarter phase accents Pluto in Aquarius and Chiron moving through Taurus. A strong possibility is that crypto-currencies will come under attack and the global financial system could once again be threatened, if not compromised.

If there is indeed yet another iceberg set to appear through these years, we would do well to have ready and easy access to non-digital reserves should a terrorist or other catastrophe knock out trading systems.

CHAPTER 5

Provisions, Experience, and Investments

Before considering potentially optimum investments, it is a useful exercise to again review your position as regards self-investment. Would you invest in you? Would others consider you to be a competent ship's master? Would they deem you capable of coping with problems on board and managing crisis? Taking stock of where you are, your expertise, and your hopes and aspirations is a most useful exercise. Forward-planning starts here.

There are some basic questions to answer. While there can be no "certain" answers, even guideline replies provide useful information. The order of these questions isn't important. It might also be the case that you answer these questions one way today and another tomorrow and in yet another next week. Note that this initial step does not take into account the potential shown in your personal horoscope but a simple "rough and ready check" and most useful template.

- Are you able to work?
- Do you want to earn?
- If you are working, are you happy?
- If you aren't working, and want to, are you marketable?
- If you aren't happy doing what you are doing now, is there another avenue you'd like to pursue in this lifetime?
- How would you rate your health and fitness?
- Are you "lucky"?
- What "stock" do you already own? NB. Stock does not have to be literal "stocks or equity," but would include marketable talents, property that could be sold if necessary, and, importantly, the good will and support you have from friends and family on the quayside.

Responding to these questions is an exercise that ought to be carried out regularly. Responses will vary from year to year.

Yet, in taking the time to consider these, you are also carrying out a basic financial health check. In the process, you might also alight on ideas worthy of at least an investment of time, if not of accrued savings.

In going through this list, you could determine time-lines: including when you want to stop working. You might also give consideration to whether or not you have developed spending or savings habits that should be improved. This might be something you discuss with your astrologer and financial advisor.

To be clear, before moving forward, careful consideration of your present position is wise! What is in your "hold"—your savings, assets, and latent talents—are the provisions on which you will rely in the coming years.

To navigate your financial journey requires that you make regular assessment of your position and condition. Analysis of your birth chart is helpful. Even rudimentary understanding of your chart and of the position of the slow moving planets as they make their way through the zodiac is helpful. You can use your chart, in consultation, to determine the approximate times when talents can be used to store provisions (savings from earnings), and when developing an investment strategy should take priority.

Natural Assets (Provisions)

Start by giving thought to the position of the Sun at your birth (your sun sign). This position gives clues as to the areas in which you are likely to "shine." It is often the case that where your talents surface, reward (usually financial) follows.

Though it appears true that those born with the Sun in either Taurus or Scorpio have obvious financial acumen, it is not the case that all the other signs have none! In some people this is a more obvious trait than in others.

Remember that a complete reading of your birth chart uses the exact, date, time and place of that event. What is offered here is a super-quick, broad brush-stroke of how the position of the Sun at birth colors a person's financial outlook.

Aries: Wants quick results and can be impetuous. Good instincts but poor at risk assessment.

Taurus: Takes a considered approach. Likes quality, is selective and appreciative of good craftsmanship.

Gemini: Likes choice and to negotiate. Often commercially astute but easily distracted.

Cancer: Careful with resources. Often collects more than they need. Good at selecting stocks that will flourish but has a tendency to over-worry.

Leo: Is attracted to "the best." Can over-spend or detach entirely from material possessions. Finds the challenge of endless trading exhausting.

Virgo: A justifiable reputation for worrying. Anxious to see books balanced and often focused on minutiae, yet is rarely over-awed by large numbers (sums of money). Tends to choose long-term investments wisely but often relentlessly questions advisors, and is prone to chopping and changing plans to their financial cost.

Libra: needs to see accounts balanced. Might take a long time to select stocks for their portfolio but tends to choose wisely. Unafraid to cut losses if necessary.

Scorpio: Sensitive. Sees value that others miss. Good at bargain hunting but also has a taste for luxury. Naturally good at bartering.

Sagittarius: Can be fiscally careless but is generally more con- servative than others suspect. Generous (sometimes to a fault) but with a natural confidence and ability to attract good fortune.

Capricorn: Cautious, prudent, risk-averse. Buys for quality and will do without until they've saved for the "right" item.

Aquarius: At times conservative and cautious, and at others cavalier and prone to crazy over-spends.

Pisces: Not quite easy come, easy go, but sensitive to the ebb and flow of finance. Can live on the tightest of budgets or drift toward realms of luxury. In investments will choose a stock for no apparently good reason but which often turns out to yield super reward.

Of course, the Moon and the planets play their part. The Sun takes priority. Its position by sign is the strongest indicator by far of where you are likely to shine and excel.

Progressed Horoscope

Though the idea of a progressed horoscope sounds complicated, it is possible to command a little elementary mastery of this technique. Consider: the Earth did not stop turning after you were born: even a few hours later, the Sun, Moon and planets continued on their silent journeys through the galaxy.

The progressed horoscope is based on a commonly used astrological technique which equates the movement of the planets every day after birth as being equivalent to one year of life. This progression of the Sun is important in the story of your life journey and is perhaps best explained with an example:

Suppose we have a friend whose birthday is July 7. We know that the Sun changes signs on or around twenty-first of each month and, very roughly, travels about one degree per day. We can then do a rough and ready calculation that your friend's natal (birth) Sun position will be around 16 Cancer. (That is, 0° Cancer begins around June 21; there are thirty days in June; so the Sun would travel nine more degrees in the month of June, and then seven more degrees to reach July 7 (9 + 7 = 16).)

Each sign contains 30 degrees. We now know that at (roughly) age 14, our friend's Cancer Sun, progressed into Leo. Thirty years later, at around age 44, it progressed into the next sign of the zodiac, Virgo.

Thus, whatever sign you were born under, the Sun will, at some stage, move on to the neighboring sign where it will stay for approximately thirty years before moving on to the next sign.

Please note that this is a very rough and ready calculation— but still an easy party-piece! Most people can relate to a change in their circumstances when the Progressed Sun moved from one sign to another.

During the years when the Sun passes through Taurus or Scorpio especially (and to a lesser degree Cancer or Capricorn, which are also promising signs for finance) you might well develop financial skill. If you have your chart read by a professional astrologer, they will also make note of when the Progressed Moon (and other planets too) move through both these signs and other areas associated with finance, and will counsel you as to optimum moments to improve latent acumen.

If we agree that some signs are better at managing money than others, we should also consider which signs appear to have least ability in this area. We might conclude that when the Sun at birth or by progression moves through one of the Mutable signs of Gemini, Virgo, Sagittarius, or Pisces, that there is likely to be insufficient attention being given to such money matters. Certainly it seems to be the case that when these signs are active, then people are so busy rushing from one thing to another, they fail to observe signals (turning points) and so often miss opportunities. Again, this is something to discuss with a financial advisor or astrological guide.

While what is offered above is a simple and thought-provoking guide, the purpose of this book is to assist you in navigating the stormy financial waters that lie ahead. To do this, we consider the effect that the position of the outer planets is likely to have on how we husband our basic provisions (natural talents) and investments.

On a daily basis we each invest in our health through eating and exercising. Financial investment does not always require this quotidian approach: there tend to be periods when financial matters have priority. This is where observation of the movement and position of the outer planets and their cycles proves useful.

In noting the planetary "gear changes" (when the slower moving planes move from one sign to another), it is possible to identify which sectors will go through greatest upheaval and which might then offer optimum reward.

Experience

A quick look at the financial pages of any newspaper reveals that businesses are grouped in sectors: for example mining, house-building, financial services, etc. In astrology, each is said to be "ruled" by a particular planet or planetary cycle. As you might imagine, when Pluto, a slow-moving planet, moves from one sign to the next, the underpinning of relevant sectors is affected negatively while other sectors are re-energized.

The most obviously affected area of business affected by Pluto's move into Capricorn was the banking industry. For many years, the banks were institutions to be trusted. It was also the case that so-called "blue chip" companies were felt to be sufficiently robust to withstand low points in the business cycle. Following the global financial crash, we learned that these institutions were not built on the solid ground that had been assumed. Moreover, we discovered that many of the household names thought to be commercially invincible were anything but: already many of these companies have disappeared from the high street.

We should expect more banks and longstanding businesses to fail before Pluto leaves Capricorn in 2024. In 2020, as many other planets group in Capricorn, some governments will feel the need to underpin those businesses and enterprises deemed essential for the common good. Though we might wonder "with what?" given that so many governments will surely have difficulty paying their own staff, let alone bailing out others. Doubtless there will be restructuring exercises and other modifications made to keep compromised businesses afloat. Those reliant on dividends from these corporations should expect to experience diminished returns—if any—as rescue operations begin.

Whereas there was a time when holding shares in blue chip companies was deemed a core or vital part of any investment portfolio, this may no longer be the case. Those choosing to invest in these generally super-large businesses should of course keep abreast of news about these companies and, if not familiar with reading financial reports, accept advice from their financial advisors about a company's security.

Though stock markets have soared since the global financial crisis, it is more than a little interesting to note that banking stocks have not followed suit. These are still bobbing along on the surface, effectively going nowhere, and are in danger of being sucked down again. Until Pluto completes its transit of Capricorn, the crisis of 2007–2008 cannot be considered to be over. Bond markets too are likely to be seriously—and adversely—affected.

Bonds are essentially long-term lending agreements. You lend money to a business for a definite period. In return, the business or the government to whom you have lent the money, promises to repay the money on a specific date. During the term of the loan, the company or business pays interest at an agreed rate. You, the lender know what that amount will be and can budget accordingly. The premise of course is that those to whom you have lent this money will repay the principal sum as agreed on the set date. Given the potential for a Great Financial Reset before Pluto leaves Capricorn, it is entirely possible that many bonds should be classified as junk. Those loans will never be repaid.

This might even be true of Treasury Bonds in the USA, where Pluto is due to return to the position held at the birth of the present day United States of America. It is known that despite increase in various US indices, with the implication that that nation is on the path to financial success, that the USA is many trillions of dollars in debt: in fact, at a level far more than it earns in any year. As with other nations, the USA may not be able to pay its bond holders.

No individual can live long enough for Pluto to return to its natal position. It's rare even for countries to achieve this. Within a 246-year period (Pluto cycle) many country borders change and new legal identities are formed. England can be used as an example of how Pluto returns are negotiated, though the chart for England (based on the Coronation of William the Conqueror on Christmas Day 1066) is not as valid now that we have a chart for Great Britain (January 1, 1801). In the former chart, Pluto was in an early degree of Pisces, a position returned to in the early fourteenth century, again in the mid sixteenth century and at the turn of the nineteenth century. The next Pluto return to the 1801 chart for the United Kingdom will be in the mid 2030s.

We can learn something from these Pluto returns: each was associated with reform of tax laws, and each was driven by government or ruling class need to repay debt. The USA government similarly may need to impose punitive taxation in an effort to repay its loans. Indeed, though many other nations are similarly over-leveraged, an inability to repay these particular loans could be one of the key features of the Great Financial Reset forecast for 2020–2022.

Those who have already lent money to either governments or big business may yet find that these institutions are unable to fulfil their obligations. The very many people who do not think that they own these bonds should be aware that their pensions are almost certainly invested in them. Even their governments may have lent to other countries who then default. Many governments may be unable to pay state pensions. It is probable they will raise the agreed pension age to delay making those payments to a later date.

If pensions cannot be relied upon, and if there is real danger of some banks collapsing—not mention the bond market, then the question must be "where can savings be held safely"? From the cosmic perspective we should look at the business sectors associated with signs which are not threatened by Pluto's Capricorn passage and are instead boosted by it.

Here we can learn from the past: when Pluto traveled through Cancer (the sign opposite Capricorn) the business sectors which fared comparatively well were Scorpio and Pisces (the other two Water signs of the zodiac). This included the banking and rebuilding sectors (Scorpio) and health, advertising and oil (all associated with Pisces). If you had held stocks in sound companies working in these sectors from Pluto's entry into Cancer and through to its exit, you would have done well.

The "winners" this time, as Pluto makes its slow journey through Capricorn, should be those associated with Taurus and Virgo (the other two Earth signs). At the time of writing, Pluto is almost two thirds of the way through its journey through Capricorn and it should be possible to see evidence of advancement in Taurus or Virgo sectors.

Taurus-related industries cover natural products: care of the environment, leather goods, emeralds, forestry, furniture, luggage, confectionery, and starchy foods. True, Taurus is also linked to banking: this though is of the very personal kind, i.e. the piggy bank, but includes businesses offering small personal loans rather than larger ones covering business capital or mortgages.

Virgo companies include those offering accounting services, discount retailers, health care products and services, all service providers (nursing care especially), and data care. Given that Pluto is the planet associated with mining, we should also be alert to opportunity for data mining companies to excel in the next few years.

There is already evidence that companies working and developing new products and services in these areas are thriving. Before investing in any of these it would, as always, be necessary to check the fundamentals of the company concerned. However, if reading this before 2021, do consider discussing these options with your financial advisor.

Personal Investment and Provisions

Though much depends on the distribution of the planets at the time and place of your birth, it is nevertheless the case that when Pluto transits your Sun sign, resources will be stretched. Just to underline the point, not everyone will experience a direct transit of Pluto through their Sun sign during their lifetimes, given that it takes that planet a quarter of a millennium to pass through all twelve signs.

We will consider just two possibilities: Pluto passing through your Sun-sign or opposing it, i.e., if you were born with the Sun in Cancer, then Pluto has opposed your sign in recent years or is about to, depending on your actual birth date. (Those born just before the Sun moved from Cancer to Leo will not experience this transit until 2023–2024.) Equally, if you were born with the Sun in Capricorn, but perhaps just a few days before the Sun moved on into Aquarius, you won't experience Pluto transiting over your natal Sun position until 2023–2024.

Many of those who have already experienced these transits (i.e. those with birthdays between June 21 and mid-July or between December 21 and mid-January), have now lived through this experience: have changed jobs, moved, and indeed, to use truly Pluto words, experienced empowerment and transformation. Though the nature of this profound change is not often immediately recognized. Pluto's passage over the natal Sun position—or at right angles, or opposed to it, can rarely be described as "pleasant": associated upheaval can be emotionally painful, physically debilitating, and mentally exhausting.

(For astrologers: when Pluto is at 90 degrees—or even 45 or 135 degrees from the birth sign the native will experience variations on this theme.)

Before the assumption is made that such transits are all "bad," I want to point out that in listening to clients stories I am struck by how Pluto transit to their Sun has marked a period of investment. True, they have not often realized that actions taken at this time would bring long-term reward, yet it may be that Pluto transits to the Sun (or indeed to the natal Moon) position, are "pension building opportunities." To be clear, decisions taken as Pluto forms these major aspects are often thought to be unworthy of note. It is only later revealed that apparently inconsequential actions have proved to be financially shrewd.

One client, going through a difficult time as Pluto moved over her Sun (in her case a divorce), bought a small painting to cheer herself up. That painting was later found to have considerable value. By the time this realization was made, Pluto had completed its transit of her sign and was well established in the next. It can be the case that it takes two decades for such an initial investment to yield reward.

This instance, and others, have convinced me of the value of looking back—with a client—at times when these aspects have taken place. During the course of the ensuing discussion together we have found "nuggets" of yet to be realized value.

At the time of writing, Pluto is moving through Capricorn. It is true that those born under this sign, or in signs opposite or square to Capricorn (the Cardinal signs of Aries, Cancer or Libra) are likely experiencing Pluto-related upheaval—but hopefully later reward. It is also true that Pluto's transit of Capricorn affects each and every one of us in our own way.

Before Pluto leaves this sign, the banking sector and the security it is supposed to provide will be tested again and again. If history repeats, then, just as in the 1930s, many banks will fail. Savings will be under threat. Finding better ways of securing these is a challenge now and will be for many years to come.

Many may be drawn to commodities (gold, silver, platinum, etc.) believing these to offer safer haven. However, these assets bring their challenges: do you invest in a fund or in the actual metal? If you choose the latter, how can it be protected? And what of governments? Might these assets be confiscated to pay their debts? It might be better to buy into precious jewels that can be stored and moved with greater ease.

It would be negligent not to refer to the fact that some individuals are forecasting the end of the world as we have known it. They fear Armageddon—not necessarily financial. I certainly have worries for global finance. It may be that such chaos is unavoidable: essential before more robust and equitable systems are put in place. It seems unthinkable that so much wealth is held by so few, and likely that as Pluto moves through Aquarius, redistribution will be an essential process.

I am confident that the best investments of all are in good friends, family, and working relationships with neighbors. Whatever happens in the coming years—without a good network, whatever the strength and quantity of your assets—your security will be compromised.

For now, let us assume that we will—though probably with some difficulty—work

through the next few years and survive Pluto's transit of the last few degrees of Capricorn.

Aquarian Provisions

Between 2024 and 2032, Pluto moves through neighboring sign of Aquarius. Whereas the banking industry experienced seismic shocks as Pluto entered Capricorn, this time it is likely to be non-government agencies (NGOs) that hit the headlines. As we saw with banking, Pluto destroys before rebuilding. It is essential—even ahead of Pluto's arrival in Aquarius—for investors to be aware of the potential losses, and even destruction likely to be experienced by Aquarius-related sectors and businesses.

Aquarius is considered to be the eleventh sign of the zodiac and is of the Fixed and Air group. Those born with the Sun in this sign often display singularity of purpose, a desire to work for the common good, and display a delightful if at times quirky sense of humor. They are also said to be natural futurologists: at times giving the impression of "coming from another planet," yet they are often the kindest and most sentimental of souls.

For individuals born with the Sun in Aquarius, the arrival of Pluto in their sign will likely not be at all comfortable. The discovery of the extent of manipulation and downright thuggery even amongst the institutions and organizations supposedly working for the benefit of those unable to look after themselves, will doubtless be especially distressing.

Companies and businesses linked to this sign will likely find—as did the banks in 2008—that their edifices are crumbling. This includes non-government organizations, mutual societies, and much of the insurance industry. Many high-tech companies, perhaps lacking sufficient capital, or where directors have withdrawn considerable dividend to the detriment of company foundations, will likely also fail after Pluto passes into Aquarius in 2023. Before that time though there are likely gains to be made.

Aquarius is often thought of as the sign associated with the "Space Age." It is probable that as Jupiter passes through this sign in 2021, great strides forward will be made in space-age technologies, robotics, and space travel. Tempting as it may be to invest in these breakthroughs, it is probable that returns will be poor if not negative after Pluto arrives in Aquarius in 2024. For a start, these enterprises may have been under-capitalized and so collapse even after showing so much early promise. It is essential to analyse the fundamentals of any company before investing. Some of these businesses will do exceptionally well. It is the whole sector that could be rendered fragile by Pluto's presence in this sector of the zodiac. The optimum period to buy into this sector may be just ahead of Jupiter's arrival in Aquarius—perhaps in late 2020 with a view to selling late in 2022 ahead of Pluto's arrival in 2024.

Pluto is associated with toxicity and pollution, and Aquarius is an Air sign. Concern for air quality will surely increase. Penalties given to those polluting the atmosphere, and lawsuits served against those businesses that have made greatest contribution to the destruction of quality air, will surely affect the share prices of many companies. It would be wise to ditch these stocks well ahead of Pluto's arrival in Aquarius in 2024, while considering investment in those businesses with proven record of improving air quality. Here in London, air-cleaning machines have been installed at one of the major London rail centers. This plan has attracted much attention: these installations may be the first of many.

As Pluto reaches Aquarius, those born under that sign should prepare for a near decade period of renewal. How tricky and demanding this is will depend much on how resistant they are to change. Those who have been through a Pluto transit to their Sun will tell you that any resistance is futile. They might even go further and suggest that the quicker you are to embrace the possibilities that come with enforced upheaval, the greater the possibility of expanding your career portfolio if not your asset base.

If you want to hear first-hand an example of a Pluto transit to a Fixed sign, then talk to relatives or friends born with the Sun in either Taurus or Scorpio who went through these transits in the 1980s. Hear their stories and learn: remembering that we are all unique and that any similarities will be due to their individual response systems and how change was accepted—or not! There is high probability that during these years these people went through enforced "reinvention."

Prior to 2023, and not without good reason, Aquarius-born individuals are likely to challenge corporate bodies and institutions to whom they have entrusted assets. An alternative would be resigning from working for these and flexing entrepreneurial muscles.

This action though might well include discussions centered on tax liabilities. Indeed, it should be considered wise to address these issues and to obtain an accurate summary of Aquarius' financial position prior to Pluto's Aquarius ingress. Please note that Pluto is associated with taxation matters of all kinds. It is not at all uncommon for those going through a Pluto transit to feel powerless in the face of a major tax audit.

Rest assured that even if you weren't born under either Capricorn or Aquarius, you will still feel the effect both of Pluto's passage through these signs and the transition from one to the other. Indeed all signs should be prepared for 2023 through 2025 to be a demanding time financially. Having reserves in place will surely be imperative. These should be diverse: if we can't trust governments and currencies, there is little point in having piles of cash stored underneath the bed!

It could be argued that having cash in more than one currency would be helpful. It might also help to have tangible items that can be sold as necessary: gold, silver, art, or whatever. Simplistic as this might be, these actions would put in place a useful safety-net.

While those with the Sun in either Capricorn and Aquarius might appear most obviously affected by developments in the financial world, their opposite signs will surely also be affected. Those born with the Sun in Cancer or Leo may find the coming years especially demanding. With the former, they may find that by 2023–2024, they need to take increased control of joint financial affairs.

A Cancer asset is the trait of good housekeeping and husbanding. Cancers seem to have an instinctive ability to save. True, this is not always obvious: they have been known to spend, spend, spend. Yet purchases, with the memories they bring, are also likely to be durable so that when there is need to "tighten the belt," items bought are shown to be good investments.

Pluto's transit through Capricorn and then Aquarius will doubtless bring situations where Cancerians feel temporarily out of control. Though clearly much depends on the individual chart and the age of the person concerned, accessing inner resources, turning a situation around, and being empowered by the process is not without the bounds of possibility. The scary thing for this group is being faced with situations over which they feel helpless. The discovery that those whom they believed to be their protectors are themselves unable to assist will be destabilizing.

Cancerians though should not doubt their ability to rebuild and reformat. Indeed, even through the potentially fraught period of 2025–2026, when global recession could make for very real—and daily—restrictions, those born under this sign are likely to make shrewd decisions and investments. Perhaps no-one understands the meaning of "essential" more than those born under this sign. By assessing the products and services needed to survive in a new world order, and building or investing in these, Cancers could yet turn around even very difficult situations.

Those born under Leo face different challenges; many born could find their situation undermined in 2023–2024 as Pluto moves into their opposite sign.

Of course Pluto is just one planet and many factors should be taken into consideration before assessing exactly how Leos might use the positive energies of Pluto's transit through Capricorn. However, it seems likely that investing in property—especially in an anticipated falling market in 2020–2021—will seem a highly attractive proposition. Full attention though must be given to PRACTICAL (Capricorn is an Earth sign) matters. Workspace or proximity to work and to health agencies must be taken into account.

CHAPTER 6

Sirens and the Waiting Lorelei of 2025

It is a rare individual who has not, at some point, been lured onto financial rocks. Very often this is a side effect of a person-to-person love affair: its end or its beginning. Occasionally it's not romance that leads the unwary into financial difficulty but desires of other kinds: houses, fast cars, etc. For a variety of reasons, the eye is taken off the financial ball—sometimes with near catastrophic results. Of course, sometimes the experience, and especially if affairs of the heart are involved, become treasured memories and the "investment" appreciated. There may be other instances, however, when a purchase is recalled with bitterness or shame and where the repercussions of loss or accrued debt have appalling and long-term impact.

It could be argued that in the run up to the global financial crash, the whole world was lured onto the financial rocks that were obvious to just a few (astrologers amongst them!). In 2004 in my original *Financial Universe* book, I explained my fears for 2007–2008 when Pluto would align with the Galactic Center before crossing from Sagittarius to Capricorn. Capricorn is the sign associated with large corporations, banking, and government. I had grave concern for the banks of nations whose edifices I feared would crumble under planetary pressure. A decade earlier while trying to determine what might bring about this debacle, I voiced to a few clients that I thought that there might be difficulties with the housing market. Little did I know that it would be the subprime market that paved the way to the ensuing crisis.

I was confident that surfacing problems in 2007–2008 would eventually be traced back to decisions taken during the 1980s. That decade began with an alignment of Jupiter and Saturn (whose cycle is recognized as being similar to a twenty-year business cycle) in an Air sign. This would be the first alignment of its kind in over two centuries. Air is all about ideas. I deduced that the ideas that took shape in the 1980s would be unproven and seen by many as "ahead of their time." By their very nature these developments would be untried and untested. That the alignment of Jupiter with Saturn coincided with Neptune's transit through Capricorn suggested to me that some of these ideas, insufficiently grounded (Capricorn being an Earth sign and Neptune with its connections with idealism), would leave a lasting and unsafe financial legacy.

Neptune's journey through Capricorn took place from the mid-80s through to the millennium. Keywords for Neptune include disillusion, deception, masking, fantasy, and, at times, corruption. As we now know, many of the weapons of mass financial destruction—including the development of the sub-prime mortgage market—were conceived during these years and within the confines of Capricorn institutions, i.e., major and, until then, respected banks and governments.

My reasoning that this transit would lay the seeds for future financial difficulties was based on linking Neptune's Capricorn transit with my study of the Neptune-Pluto cycle of 496 years. Though this is the approximate period from one conjunction to the next, within that long period there are five sub-periods. These sub-periods are measured from one parallel aspect between the two planets and the next. Parallel aspects differ from conjunctions (where the latter share the same zodiac degree), in that they are measured from the time when the two planets are equidistant and on the same side of the celestial equator. The combined forces of one of these sub-cycles, together with the signs of the zodiac in which the two planets were traveling, led me to think that Neptune would first make gentle—and probably mesmerizing waves in the financial markets—but that these would become tumultuous and dangerous once Pluto made its Capricorn ingress.

Jupiter and Saturn form conjunctions approximately every twenty years and do so in distinct sequence. Over a period of 240 years, these conjunctions occur in one element (Fire, Earth, Air, or Water) before moving to the next—though there is often a slight overlap as one element gives way to the next. For example, in the seventeenth and eighteenth centuries, most of the Jupiter-Saturn conjunctions were in Fire signs, with the exception of two in the mid-seventeenth century which were in Water signs. These Fire sign conjunctions gave way to a series of Earth sign conjunctions beginning in 1802 and lasting through to the year 2000, with the exception of the 1981 conjunction in Air sign Libra which heralded the series beginning in 2020. It was during the twenty years of that Air-sign Libra conjunction that ideas developed which will, no doubt, eventually be linked to those of the new series (the first of these being known as a Grand Mutation).

It was always likely that development of business and financial ideas during the 1980 and 1990s would yield clues as to the direction of faster development in these areas when the Air series proper begins in 2020. As we now know, many weapons of mass financial destruction came into being as this cycle got underway, and while Neptune moved through Capricorn: the combined effect coinciding with the development of credit default swaps and of the sub prime mortgage market.

The massive debts accumulated have yet to be paid off. Neither quantitative easing applied in the United States, nor the austerity measures in other parts of the world have resolved this situation.

The financial icebergs that lie ahead—and which could see many financial institutions scuppered—will likely appear after December 2020 when Jupiter and Saturn form their next conjunction. But they will inflict their greatest damage in 2025–2026 when, I fear, the world will experience a major recession.

In 2026, Saturn and Neptune form a conjunction. This is part of their regular thirty-five-year cycle, but even more important than usual as it takes place at precisely 0° Aries: arguably the most powerful degree of the zodiac. This degree marks the date when the Sun crosses the celestial equator, the beginning of a new season. At least one astrologer has termed this the "human degree," though others term the two equinoxes and the two solstice points, the "World Axis."

Though the Sun marks each angle of the World Axis as it arrives at each equinox and solstice, of equal importance are those dates when the planets arrive at these degrees. The effect of Pluto's arrival at one of these axis points in 2008 coincided with the Global Financial Crisis. (Pluto has a reputation for removing the underpinning!) No less important are those dates when other slow-moving planets cross these points. The fact that Saturn and Neptune arrive at the apex of this axis simultaneously is remarkable, and suggests that 2026 will require, like 2008, its own special financial history yearbook.

In the last two centuries, phases in the Saturn-Neptune cycle have coincided with a rise in socialism. At their conjunction in 1846, the Communist Manifesto was published. At another, in 1917, the Bolsheviks overthrew the Russian government. No less important are the half-way points of this cycle: at their opposition phase in 1989, the Berlin Wall came down. It is entirely reasonable to assume that a swing against republicanism or conservatism will be evident in the mid-2020s. Coinciding with Pluto's Aquarius ingress, a wave of disquiet about inequality and a desire to redistribute wealth is likely to lead to political chaos in many parts of the world as governments with more right-wing bent are overthrown.

For much of the twentieth century, oil prices have been a barometer of economic activity. It is interesting that the hard phases in the Saturn-Neptune cycle (i.e. the conjunction, square, and opposition) have coincided with dips in oil prices. If history repeats, then the mid-2020s could find oil prices at a near all-time low.

It is not difficult to view the conjunction of Saturn with Neptune as a dark rain cloud or looming dark wave, and hard to find the positives in what could be a prolonged and difficult period for many. Given that this time is likely to bring the roughest of seas (as outlined in chapter four: reference points), the task for investors in 2025 will be to either find shelter for their assets and savings—or find a market for icebergs!

Yet the planets do move on. The conjunction is not a permanent feature. Saturn, moving faster than Neptune, will separate from this aspect, and within a few years the two planets will be in an acknowledged positive phase. With the high probability of assets losing value through these years and with increasing concern about the spread of disease, the most valuable assets will surely be friends, family, and collections or art that bring pleasure while also being viewed as heirlooms.

As was the case in 2008, some individuals will surely experience a financial drowning in 2025 while others make near miraculous escapes. Still others may already be well-placed to jump into the life boats. The purpose of this chapter is to identify those who might best survive, how we can all learn from past financial error, and how different generations might position themselves so that they can avoid the worst.

Neptune Generations

Just as we saw in the opening chapter that Pluto's position by sign alerts us to different operating engines and how they are best maintained, so Neptune's position at birth gives clues as to how and when the call of the sirens are irresistible to either market sectors or to particular age groups.

The position of Neptune in the birth chart is valuable in identifying the best ways that each Neptune generation can ensure that their financial engines run smoothly. Looking ahead however, we can use Neptune's position by sign to identify the type of challenges likely to appear, and go further by observing major planetary configurations involving Neptune that will form. Whereas the sign alerts us to the type of problem ahead, when Neptune is part of a major midpoint configuration, we learn something of the damages we may face and the sectors most likely to be affected. Moreover, through understanding the different "Neptune generations" we can also identify which are most likely to end up on the rocks and when. Hopefully, this "foreknowledge" will be sufficient to alert these people to avoid catastrophe.

We know to avoid putting oil in a diesel engine car—but occasionally may experience that kind of misadventure. In planetary terms, this is most likely to occur when Neptune is at an angle to its natal position, or to the position of the Sun, Moon, or significant planet in the natal chart. This is when many people make such an error: a costly, and occasionally financially-catastrophic mistake. Though this work cannot cover every eventuality, we can consider those times when whole generations (as defined by Neptune's position at sign) will likely be lured onto financial rocks.

Neptune is a slow moving planet, taking 164 years to tour the zodiac. Even though we now live longer, it is unlikely that you will live long enough for Neptune to return to the position it held at birth. The "hard" aspects it makes, i.e. when it is forty-five degrees, right angles, or opposes its natal position, are the most difficult.

Since its discovery in the mid-nineteenth century, Neptune's astrological role has connected it with all that is ethereal, mystical, unseen, and unquantifiable. The effect of a piece of art cannot always be explained or calibrated. Equally, Neptune's role in the world of finance doesn't lend itself to easy quantification. This planet has been associated with fraud and evasion of fiscal responsibility. Yet Neptune is often part of a planetary picture in the charts of the mega rich who may be innocent of any financial wrong-doing; showing instead an instinct to attract and accumulate wealth. Neptune is slippery, yet enchanting and seductive, and, for some people, brings apparently limitless wealth.

It is associated with the film industry where it is not unknown for an actor to be paid vast sums while other actors, unnoticed, struggle to make ends meet. It seems that when Neptune is involved, it is either "all" or "nothing."

Knowing Neptune's position at birth assists in understanding why particular groups of people are seduced by certain types of art and, indeed, certain products and services. Equally, knowledge of Neptune's position at a company's inception gives clues as to how far a company might grow. The position of Neptune at any given moment tells us much about aspirations and visions of the future.

Neptune is also linked to advertising and the world of media. Under a "bad" Neptune aspect you may be talked about negatively, or a product or service receive bad press. Equally, a well-placed Neptune can lead to word of mouth free advertising.

Like the Internet, the Neptune-effect goes well beyond usual boundaries. Products bought on one side of the world can be transported with ease and resold in another continent at quite different price to that announced at company headquarters.

Neptune's clarion call might at first sound curious. Before long, the sound becomes ever more compelling, drawing the unwary toward various kinds of disaster.

As with Pluto, each time Neptune crosses into a sign, there is change of trend. It has journeyed through just six signs of the zodiac since 1940: two Air and two Water signs, and just one Earth and one Fire sign.

In considering each of these groups and their financial development we can also forecast probable future behavior. This is important. Before identifying which sectors might do well in the coming years, we also need to know the likelihood of a particular group doing adequate risk assessment before investing in these.

- Libra (Air) 1940–September 56
- Scorpio (Water) September 1956–August 1970
- Sagittarius (Fire) August 1970–June 1984
- Capricorn (Earth) June 1984–March 1998
- Aquarius (Air) March 1998–November 2011
- Pisces (Water) November 2011–2025

Neptune in Libra (1940–1956)

People born between 1940 and 1956 have Neptune in Libra—one of the Air signs—and are generally seduced by ideas. Where investing is concerned, they are lured by the idea of getting in on the "ground floor." Some are inveterate investors in young businesses. It's interesting that during their lifetimes, governments have often offered tax incentives to this group if they would invest in start-ups. To do this requires confidence and shared vision.

Many of this generation are already of retirement age and are dealing with the frailties that come with age. A new expense for this group centers on health and health-related products (but yes, more than a few have been known to spend money on cruises!).

Assuming that there is still some cash available to invest, the lure of products that boost health will surely be considerable. They might also be attracted to those companies providing services which are thought to be of long-term benefit to mankind. Examples here would be sea and solar power, or anything that cleans up the oceans or brings clean and pure water to those without easy access to it. Commendable as all this may be, those with Neptune in Libra need to check and double check that the companies with whom they wish to invest funds do have the necessary capital and—above all—the technical and administrative ability to see the demand for their products and services increase.

The ubiquitous rise of products that promise much but have yet to be fully tested could be such that many with Neptune in Libra are lured to lose their investments (similar to the dot-coms but from these other sectors).

Many of this group will likely discover that the funds they thought were safely set aside for their later lives are wholly inadequate. We should not, of course, overlook the fact that many of these people also have Pluto in Leo, and that faced with this challenge, they are as likely to dig deep, rediscover their latent entrepreneurial abilities, and start up new ventures.

Many though will not be in this possibly envious position. Theirs could be a gloomy future—especially if ill-health precludes them from working post-retirement age. There is no "easy" solution to their dilemma, though it may be helpful to alert them to the difficulties ahead in 2025, and to suggest that by then they are known to those organizations able to help those in need. In building up their own friendship networks, too, they may find ways to join forces and reduce costs.

Few of us are in a position to invest much before our early 20s at the earliest, so we can discount the transits of Neptune through Scorpio and Sagittarius when those born with Neptune in Libra were too young to make long-term financial investment.

Rather we will focus on those years when Neptune had advanced three signs—to Capricorn, (another Cardinal sign). The planet was then at right-angle to Neptune's position in Libra. Many of those with this placement chose to invest in what would become known as the "dot-coms." Through those years, these companies seemed to show so much promise. Yet they often proved siren calls, and some investors lost money in the dot-com crash of 2000. The problem here was that those with Neptune in Libra were captivated by the idea but, in many cases, failed to do the background checks to ensure that the companies were sufficiently capitalized. In a sense, their Neptunian "Air"—combined with Neptune's transit through Earthy Capricorn—whipped up such a storm that financial radars failed to warn of impending crisis.

Though this is obviously a generalization—as personal charts must be taken into account—many of those born with Neptune in Libra were taken in by the commercial ideas presented as Neptune moved through Aquarius from 1998 to 2011. Some forgot the lessons of the 1990s and were once again swept up in a wave of enthusiasm for the ideas developing in the first decade of the new millennium. It is only now, as Neptune moves through Watery Pisces, that they are learning that many of those concepts have morphed into something entirely different to what was initially envisaged. Of course they may yet make gain—much will depend on the actual company and the fundamentals behind it.

Broadly though, and before Neptune moves into Aries (the opposite sign to Libra) in 2024, this age group should undertake careful risk-assessment of investments made between 1998 and 2011. It may be time to move into other areas.

Neptune in Scorpio (1956–1970)

Of course much happens in any year and isolating any one commercial development does not give a clear picture. As Neptune moved from Libra to Scorpio in 1956, many people were bewildered (a Neptune word) by a new product brought to market: the IBM mainframe computer. This was a key development on the road to the information highway with which we are now so familiar. It is unlikely that those who invested in this remarkable development were disappointed. With the dawn of the computing age, new markets opened up.

Those who invested in those initially huge machines could

never have imagined that one day so many of us would wander around with pocket sized computers with greater power than those first mainframes. Neither, presumably, would they have imagined the extraordinary number of products and services that have since developed.

Those born with Neptune in Scorpio are, however, exceptions to this rule. This group, though obviously unaware of the full potential, nevertheless had an instinct that this sector might yet bring fabulous reward. I have clients born with Neptune in Scorpio whose focus is on security, surveillance, and protection. When they became of age to invest, and through the 1990s as Neptune moved through Capricorn, they were alert to opportunities in these markets.

It is also true that a few from this generation saw the potential of the "dark web." These are not my clients! Nevertheless it is easy to understand the lure of wealth through nefarious activities in an unlegislated area of the world wide web. That these people saw their capital grow is probable. They could yet come unstuck as legislation and tightening of controls makes it harder to operate. Though the tips of these icebergs are now visible, it is likely that the full effect—and potential shipwrecks—will occur once Saturn enters Aquarius. Saturn will then form a right angle (square) to the Neptune position of those born with Neptune in Scorpio. For those with this placement, risk management and security should be a priority between 2020 and 2022.

People born with the Sun in the sign of Scorpio seem to have natural financial acumen. Those with Neptune in this sign usually have that talent—although if it is not recognized, then they imagine having it. Often this law of attraction works. As Neptune makes its passage through Pisces (another of the Water signs) until 2024, this group should have no difficulty in identifying stocks and sectors with potential for growth. The key here though is playing for the long-term. Under this promising aspect (Neptune making a trine from one Water sign to another), growth appears to work best when allowed to happen unrestrained, i.e., those who buy into stocks looking for long-term gain are likely best poised to make profit. Quick gains are unlikely.

As is common, when Neptune had moved 90° from its initial, or natal, starting point and began its transit of Aquarius, many of those born with Neptune in Fixed sign Scorpio experienced financial seduction and loss. However, this transit also coincided with Uranus' transit of Pisces. For a few months, Uranus was in a sign preferred by Neptune, and Neptune in one preferred by Neptune. This situation is termed "mutual reception" and, in many ways, causes the waters to be muddied.

During this extraordinary period, two sectors appeared to cross-fertilize: technology and advertising. The development of tools that allowed the geo-targeting of advertisements on the Internet occurred at breathtaking speed and the value of certain stocks soared (e.g., Facebook).

I had clients born with Neptune in Scorpio who were super-alert to the possibilities and bought into this and similar stocks during this heady period. And yes, they made extraordinary gain. It is significant that the two clients from this group who have kept me posted on their trades, both chose to sell this stock before Saturn left Sagittarius and were unaffected by recent losses.

Neptune in Sagittarius (1970–1984)

Perhaps more than any other group, those born with Neptune in Sagittarius have a tendency to believe that they can "get rich quick." It should be recalled that they grew up during the "Yuppie" era of easy credit. We might agree that many of the role models of this period did not set good examples. Yet some of those born with Neptune in Sagittarius have already realized early financial goals.

Neptune is the planet of possibilities and fantasies, while Sagittarius is naturally optimistic. It is probably true that the first stage of realizing a dream is to have a vision of success. As a generalization, those with Neptune in Sagittarius are fortunate in that they seem to have no difficulty at all in creating that vision of wealth.

Clearly much—MUCH—depends on each individual chart. What can be said is that since 2008, when Neptune began its slow journey through Pisces (90 degrees from Sagittarius and a transit that does not conclude until 2024), those of this generation, brought up on easy credit, have had to learn the hard way that credit is only available to those who have built up good ratings. Trust and goodwill are not enough!

Pisces, like Sagittarius, is another of the Mutable signs. It is easy then for those born with Neptune in the latter sign to be derailed by apparently fantastic opportunity that comes to naught. Until 2024, those born with Neptune in Sagittarius should be careful not to be blown off financial course by ideas (products or services) that are not yet proven. In particular, they should consider steering clear of media, advertising, pharmaceutical, and oil stocks. They could as easily be seduced by some of the new bio-medical products which are as yet unproven. Only those with fiscal discipline (a term not often used in relation to Neptune in Sagittarius) should play in these markets. They are likely to prove too dangerous for those without this self-restraint.

It is fascinating to note that it was during Neptune's passage through Sagittarius that international loan agreements increased in volume. With this came the credit default swaps that few of us even knew existed until the bubble burst as Pluto moved into Capricorn in 2008.

At the individual level, the financial paths of those born with Neptune in Sagittarius have been slippery to say the least. By the time of the global financial crisis, some of these people were only just reaching their early 20s, often not yet in work, and so unable to build up the much-needed credit profile on which loans depend. A few may not reach their desired credit rating until Neptune reaches Gemini in the 2040s, though most could improve their situation when both Jupiter and Saturn pass through Air-sign Aquarius between December 2020 and November 2021. Remember: fire loves air!

Those who have managed to achieve good credit rating should be well placed to surf the tumultuous waves of 2023–2024. Indeed, by the time that Neptune reaches the next Fire sign (Aries in 2025), these individuals should find warm investment currents. Unlike many others, they might see their investments grow alongside their ever-improving credit rating.

Neptune in Capricorn (1984–1998)

Neptune is associated with Water and Capricorn is one of the Earth signs. The mix of the two can form malleable and useful clay. To create a water-tight pot though requires that the structure is non-porous and the design attractive and practical. Bringing these requirements together demands expertise: whether the finished product is achieved through machine manufacture or by hand.

If Neptune is thought of as the oil in our financial engine, then its position in Capricorn suggests an oil that has long tradition. It may not be exciting. It may not be best for Formula One racing, but it is good for reliability. This is oil that focuses on lubrication and smooth running: the essentials of everyday life.

It is perhaps not surprising then that those born with Neptune in Capricorn have learned that wherever possible it's best to buy quality and, preferably, a known brand. Individuals with Neptune in this sign value a proper receipt—and with a guarantee they know will be honored.

The downside here is that it is all too easy for those with Neptune in Capricorn to assume that so-called "household names" (often blue chip companies) will be around forever and will never default. Already some have had experience of being disabused of this notion. It is probable that many more will experience similar disillusionment in the first half of the next decade, when many of these establishments may be forced to file for bankruptcy.

A large proportion of those with Neptune in Capricorn have incurred a mountain of debt while in pursuit of higher education. Some feel that the prospect of owning their own home (a Capricorn ambition) is on permanent hold, and that they will never be able to save enough for the deposit let alone obtain a mortgage. It is perhaps true that many of these individuals feel they have already been lured onto the financial rocks and, indeed, despair of ever getting free. The very idea of being in a position to invest seems laughable to some born with this Neptune placement. Even the apparently successful entrepreneurs from this group have experienced loss on occasion—most notably through crowd-funding schemes that were well marketed, but which were not sufficiently well under-pinned by sound business planning.

It is arguably true that we all learn from experience. The "sad" part here is that as Neptune moves through Aries (and will then be at right angle to their natal Capricorn Neptune position), many of this group will choose not to invest. They may ignore these mediums—when, if took the time to check and double check the business plan, there might well be a crowd-funding scheme with real potential. If the "icebergs" or challenges for this group are in the sectors outlined above, then perhaps they could avoid these and instead focus on an area where Neptune in Capricorn could work very well: the hotel and service industries related to the opposite sign, Cancer. Opposites often attract and in this instance could yet prove to be winning areas for this generation.

The danger period for the Neptune in Capricorn generation will likely come in 2025 as Neptune makes passage through Aries. To avoid this, it is imperative that they think differently. They could consider relatively "young" companies employing craftspeople who are gaining reputation for excellent service.

It would be wholly wrong though not to recognize that it's those from this group who are very likely to see the value in investing in artificial intelligence and computer security. Indeed, where cyber-security is concerned, this group may well be either active in its development or—aware of how these products could benefit their lives—choose to invest in those developing these services, confident that they will soon be regarded as "must haves."

Neptune in Aquarius 1998–2011

Neptune reached Aquarius in 1998 leaving there in late 2011. Most of those born with Neptune in this area of the zodiac have yet to find their financial engines. Those who have located them are no doubt still in the process of discovering what does what, and what button should be pushed, and when. Even the youngest of this group are, through constant advertising bombardment, learning that there is credit to be had (at cost) and that financial matters are a complex area.

Many are already distrustful of financial institutions having seen the concern that their parents, and other trusted elders expressed when discussing money matters. Without knowing why their parents (who endured the fallout of the global financial crash) have the attitudes they do, they may nevertheless see financial matters as an abstract area to be pondered more closely at another—much later—date.

This would be unfortunate. It is probable that the natural oil this group would apply to keep their financial engines running could yet be perfect for the next two decades. It is after all this group who are growing up with smart TVs and phones and with developing artificial intelligence products. These are viewed as "normal" in their world. Naturally able to keep abreast of developments, they may choose to use inspired (Neptune) intelligence (Aquarius) to identify products and services needed in a new age.

A key period for this generation will be December 2020–2022 when Saturn moves through Aquarius. At some point (dependant on their actual birthdate), Saturn will pass Neptune's position at their birth. Though most of us live long enough to experience this transit—which can coincide with anything from experiencing a common cold, to feeling out of sorts, or weighed down by responsibilities and variations on this—for this particular group a side effect may be consolidating their long-term vision. They may realize that it really is the case that they need to start saving for their old age while in the very earliest years of their working lives.

It is of course probable that this group will be wholly unfamiliar with cash as the rest of us have known it. They will have grown up in the financial digital age, paying with their phones or through debit cards—or, by the time you read this, other as yet unlaunched systems. Without connection with physical cash, this generation will have to find new ways of measuring their day to day wealth.

A strong possibility is that they will accrue points, vouchers, or some other yet-to-be-developed token of promise. These items may well come to market post the Jupiter-Saturn conjunction in Aquarius in December 2020, but they have roots that go back to 1995–2000 as Pluto began its journey through Sagittarius. Companies formed during that earlier period will likely have an ethical code and philosophy that the Neptune in Aquarius generation senses will stand them in good stead.

Neptune in Pisces (2011–2024)

Neptune entered Pisces in 2011. The oldest of this generation are a long way from controlling of their finances! There is no service history available. In a sense, theirs are pristine financial engines, still not finished or ready for use. Their "trial" runs have yet to begin. Their financial coming of age won't begin until at least 2031, by which time the financial world will be very different.

It will also be clear to this generation, as with the earlier one with Neptune in Aquarius, that it is imperative to start saving early. They will surely also be aware of the benefits of building a portfolio of careers.

It is probable then that those with Neptune in Pisces will be sensitive to even slight changes in the tone and pitch of finance. In short, they'll be quick to move their money to areas offering better promise.

Industries associated with Pisces cover anything related to water. Those with Neptune in Pisces might well decide to invest in commercial enterprises connected to the seas, oceans, lakes, and rivers. Perhaps oil, pharmaceuticals, alcohol, beauty products, mental and spiritual health, the Internet (as mentioned above), or media, film, and advertising. Yes, this covers many, many companies. But it is fitting that those with Neptune in Pisces will likely spread their investment risk.

While still too young to have direct experience of loans and their management, their elders have been living through a period when interest rates have been exceptionally low. Indeed, these fell sharply slightly ahead of Neptune's move into Pisces. The sudden drop in rates—though clearly linked to the aftershocks of the global financial crisis—could also be explained by another quirky feature known as mutual reception. When two planets are in signs said to be ruled by the other, they "swap places" and act as though they were in their preferred sign. Uranus (planet of the unexpected) was in mutual reception with Neptune from just after the global crash: at which point interest rates sank.

Positive as this experience has been for borrowers, it has not been a good time for savers. They have seen savings dwindle. Some may even have heard their elders talking about the actual cost of having a bank account in the first place. Some accounts have had a monthly charge just to operate. Yet some of the elders have been "anaesthetized" by these low rates—especially if they had little experience of borrowing a large sum (for a mortgage perhaps). When rates rise—as they will—such people may have real difficulty in meeting their obligations.

Those with Neptune in Pisces might initially be mystified and confused—and perhaps even wonder how their elders could not have seen these rocks (rising interest rates) looming. We can be reasonably confident that when it comes the time for this group to take on debt, they won't commit to variable rates, and will instead choose loan agreements that are fixed over long periods—perhaps even beyond their lifetimes.

Key Alignments

This chapter has discussed on Neptune's role as a potential fraud-ster, siren, or distractor. Neptune is presently passing through Pisces but will move into the next sign, Aries in 2024. Its last transit of a Fire sign (1970s to early 80s) included an eighteen month period when stocks lost forty percent of their value and when inflation was rampant. Interest rates rose and, with the cost of borrowing high, it was extremely difficult for new businesses to get off the ground. It is reasonable to assume a similar scenario after Neptune makes Aries ingress in 2025, and before it leaves that sign in the mid 2030s.

Before Neptune reaches Aries, it would be wise for all to secure low, long-term interest loan rates where possible. Low rates apply to savings too, however, so that while it is advisable to show a commitment to save (bankers tend to approve of this behavior), it is equally important to invest in areas offering better returns.

As we shall see in the next chapter—Full Speed Ahead—there are many areas to consider. Here we are concerned though with potential financial banana skins—which Neptune generation is most likely to experience these pratfalls, and when.

At the time of writing, Uranus is 45 degrees from Neptune. This cycle, which began in the early 1990s, has a total synodic duration of a little under 200 years. The conjunction itself is viewed as being a "seed" moment. Uranus is associated with innovation, and Neptune with imagination. It is not difficult to see that the concept and growth of social media platforms, which took root in the early 1990s as the internet gained traction, has grown exponentially since then. Those who invested in this area have seen their capital grow.

At this point in the Uranus-Neptune cycle, a crisis point has been reached. It is now seen that legislation to secure and protect will be necessary. Whenever Saturn reaches the midpoint of these two planets, we should anticipate that related companies will have to spend more on defensive measures. Their profits will no doubt be affected. Investors born with Neptune in either Libra or Sagittarius could be negatively affected if their share prices fall or dividends are much reduced.

Though these stocks could be under pressure in January 2021, arguably the most dangerous time would be those few weeks when Saturn is positioned at the midpoint of Uranus and Neptune: in February 2024, and again through August and September 2028, and March 2029.

Icebergs on the Horizon

There are six dangers warranting particular attention:

1. In December 2020, coinciding with the Jupiter-Saturn conjunction mentioned, Neptune has a prominent role. There is high probability that this will mark the start of larger interest rate rises. Those already stretched through their mortgage commitments could find this a very real strain indeed. Businesses seeking capital may find that they need far, far more than originally envisaged. Equally disturbing is that those longstanding enterprises which have, perhaps, not kept up to date with their internet security, could find themselves vulnerable to hacking—thus losing not just Christmas sales, but forfeiting the good will and trust of previously loyal customers. This problem will likely see some fall into bankruptcy early in 2021.

2. Another wave of default is probable in January 2022. This could be a very difficult period for the oil industry and at least one pharmaceutical company. The planetary picture that month also suggests industrial fraud. Such fraud is as likely to affect social media platforms as these other sectors. Companies working in these areas may find their share prices falling considerably.

3. One of the largest areas of concern will likely appear in 2022. People in many countries may be engulfed by a large wave of government demands: rising taxes and interest rates combining to create appalling financial obstacles. Once again, viral attacks on systems will surely create chaos and possibly cause some share prices to collapse altogether. The social media sector will be the most vulnerable.

4. In 2023, Jupiter, Saturn, and Pluto each change signs. We recognize that these sign changes often coincide with turbulent financial seas. True, Jupiter changes signs annually. That its Taurus ingress coincides with Saturn's move into Pisces (a Water sign) and Pluto's to Aquarius (an Air sign) suggests high winds, and wild waves. At the same time,

the two planets whose cycle is oft regarded as the "wealth cycle," Jupiter and Pluto, reach first quarter phase (i.e. Jupiter is 90 degrees ahead of Pluto). This could be described as "make-or-break." The aspect is exact on May 18—just a day after the New York Stock Exchange birthdate. The chart for the NYSE solar return will be dominated by this aspect. Anticipate power struggles and disquiet about capitalization. Mid-year we may also learn of the vulnerability of many pension funds.

5. In 2025 both Saturn and Neptune move into Aries, and mid-year Jupiter moves into Cancer. These are both Cardinal signs. We should expect that those born under similar signs (Aries, Cancer, Libra, and Capricorn) will be challenged to secure their homes (Jupiter in Cancer) while defending (Saturn) them, even as the value of these homes—and other securities—begin to fall (Neptune). It should be clear in 2025 that the world is headed toward recession. Security and protection of assets will likely dominate much conversation. Neither is it inconceivable that many will fear the outbreak of war. Uncomfortable and abhorrent as it may be to many, this brings with it the potential to invest in military hardware and in the security sector.

6. The Saturn-Neptune cycle has an approximate length of 35 years: their conjunctions forming a pattern over several centuries. That their conjunction in 2026 is at 0 degrees Aries, a degree often referred to as the Aries point or World Axis, suggests that the dawn of this particular cycle will be of great import. Please note that this event coincides with the lunar node moving through Aquarius: regarded as being the low point in the business cycle. While 2026 will likely prove a critical financial period for all, it should also be remembered that this should also be the year for extraordinary investment opportunity. We can all be financially astute with the benefit of this information and be ready and prepared to seize opportunities to restock our holds at bargain prices.

CHAPTER 7

Full Speed Ahead

Taking Control of Your Investments.

This work is intended to be a PRACTICAL GUIDE. It is hoped we have spent enough time investigating the "dark side." This last chapter is where we look at investment opportunities and the ability to enjoy safe passage on our various financial journeys.

In the opening chapter I wrote about the impact that solar activity could have on the next decade. While being a factor over which we have no control, this was something to be factored into contingency planning. As I also said, building a good network of friends and neighbors will likely be the most valuable investment any of us can make. Considerable attention was given to the awesome planetary alignment of December 2020, the coincidence of ingresses in 2023–2025, the new and important Saturn-Neptune cycle of 2026, and the difficulties of the few years beyond that.

There is, of course, no option other than to negotiate these challenges. The astro-radar system offered in this book should at the very least assist you in navigating storms and avoiding financial icebergs. Here are just a few final thoughts before moving to Full Speed Ahead.

A Special Date

My experience with clients suggests that investment and budgeting plans made between one's actual birthday and personal financial year-end carry a momentum that reduces after the year end has been reached. To be clear, there seems to be an impetus to feel "in financial charge" by the year end (presumably because of the tax penalties that would be encountered if this work is not done.) This impetus can be lost when the pressure of meeting your end of year deadlines is in the past. This has obvious dangers. There can be so much relief in having paperwork and filing up to date, and tax matters completed, that loss of attention brings the very real danger of drifting into unexpected financial problems.

For those who want to rise to the challenge of achieving optimum financial control, the period between end of (tax) year and the next birthday can and should be used as a period of accumulation. Expenses are generally easier to control after taxes have been paid. A more relaxed approach to financial matters results in cash flowing inward that then allows space and time for making investments.

Clearly these statements must be viewed as generalizations. I have studied hundreds but not thousands of charts, and have yet to subject the ones that I have studied to statistical analysis. Even so, I believe that the aforementioned annual date planning has value.

Mars

As you might imagine, knowing the position of Mars—the planet associated with direction and energy—and understanding its cycle and rhythms is important before operating at full steam ahead.

It takes Mars a little under two years to travel through the zodiac. Not only is it useful to know where it was at your birth, but also to know its position at your birthday and the year-end in question—not to mention where it is today. Just as it makes a difference if your birthday is a New Moon (or an eclipse), so it makes a difference if Mars was in the same sign as the Sun at your birth or birthday (when the Sun returns to the position it held at your birth)—or at year end (tax or personal). It may be helpful for you to complete this short table:

Mars by sign at birth	was it retrograde?
Mars' position today	is it retrograde?
Mars' position at Financial Year End	will it be retrograde?
Mars' position at your birthday this year	will it be retrograde?

Don't assume that retrograde Mars is "bad." It isn't. It simply provides a different kind of energy and requires a different type of care (much as cooking with gas or electricity require different controls). All that needs to be remembered is that when Mars is retrograde, energy can be distorted, prone to sudden bursts, and harder to keep in control. It is interesting that in global markets, there is an increase in price change during Mars retrograde periods—often described as volatility—and that as a result, the unwary investor can be adversely affected.

The so-called "red" planet brings energy to the chart. When it moves through the sign occupied at your birth, and the one after, then the impetus to improve conditions usually results in determined action. There is focus and clear aim. It can, however, be an expensive time: cash can burn a hole in your pocket when the desire to trade and see action takes hold.

Equally, when Mars moves through the sign opposite your Sun-sign, and the sign after that, it is likely to be others who do the spending on your behalf: usually by talking you into a joint investment. Of course you might be quite happy about this: perhaps you are one of those people who like others to make financial decisions.

Back-testing is a valuable exercise. Exactly how have these transits affected you in the past? Can you reprogram your reactions?

To be clear, as Mars makes passage through four particular areas of your chart (these areas are determined by the position of the Sun at your birth), your financial affairs should be watched with care: your own (sun) sign, the one that follows it, your opposite sign, and the one that follows that. It is not at all uncommon for individuals to need financial support as Mars comes to the end of these transits—or as it then transits the third sign, to need extended credit to deal with accrued debt or to cover losses.

Mars spends longer in some signs than others thanks to the retrograde periods dictated by our geocentric perspective. The weeks when Mars is retrograde should always be noted. It is not the case that markets (equities) move into reverse. But it is very likely that over the days when Mars appears to stand still prior to turning retrograde, there are significant and often negative movements. It is as though traders offer a resistance to the pending change in energy and effectively shift gear as a result. That process tends to result in prices going down and then moving wildly during the retrograde period.

Of course, knowing exactly when the financial current might turn has value. If you miss Mars' retrograde station, you can be reasonably confident that the tide will likely turn again when Mars reaches its direct station (all dates given in Appendix 9). As always, it is important to remember that you shouldn't trade with this knowledge alone. But if it compliments the results shown through technical analysis, Mars' position can provide an extra and very valuable nugget of information.

Another option is for long-term investors to look the other way and ignore any fluctuations; being reasonably confident that all will work out well later. Others may choose to see Mars retrograde periods—especially the direct station (when Mars once again seems to stand still prior to moving forward)—as potential buying opportunities.

It is also worthwhile being aware of those periods when Mars is "out of bounds," i.e., it is beyond the Sun's degree of maximum declination. Markets tend to "go wild" during these periods. Those selling as Mars reaches maximum declination are rarely disappointed. Obviously much depends on when they made their actual purchase. However, there is high probability of realizing significant profit here as prices tend to fall when Mars then comes within bounds. (Dates are given in Appendix 10.)

Crash Cycle

You may also have read elsewhere about the "Crash Cycle." This is a result of the relationship between Mars and Uranus. Research reveals that markets often fall—sometimes dramatically—after the opposition of these two planets, or sometimes when the square or right-angle aspect between them is reached. The opposition aspect occurs at least once every couple of years and it is striking how often indices turn down after the aspect is exact. To make it a little more complicated however, both the heliocentric and geocentric aspects should be marked in your trading diary as either has been known to coincide with a market top. Due to retrograde motion, it is possible for Mars to oppose Uranus a few times over the space of a few months. Again these Mars/Uranus dates are listed in Appendix II.

Going Forward

In moving full steam ahead, you could choose to move to maximum throttle in the weeks leading up to these aspects: assuming of course that you are skilled at operating your financial engine. If not, you could hit financial rocks. To use these aspects as your trading strategy without expert advice would be folly.

However, if you have adequate stops or safeguards in place, and are assured that your broker will make the sales on the date requested, AND that technical analysis is supporting your thinking, then yes, this strategy should bring reward.

Mars-Saturn Cycle

We should also note an important "stop" signal as Mars moves through the zodiac. Mars forms a conjunction with Saturn every couple of years. If Mars represents energy, and Saturn is thought of as a rock, then this alignment may imply a huge rock in the ocean that could cause great harm. Such a rock is rarely hidden from view: it is usually all-too-visible from some distance away. The Mars-Saturn rock is so obvious, and the current around it so easily gauged, that if one pays attention, the danger can be avoided.

It is important to note that each of these conjunctions take place in different signs and that the area in which the conjunction takes place is important. While it takes Mars approximately thirty months to tour the twelve signs of the zodiac, it takes Saturn almost thirty years. To compare one of these conjunctions with another in the same sign (though it will not be at the exact same degree), requires us to look back over several decades. In doing that—and though we may find another Mars-Saturn conjunction in the same sign—we also have to acknowledge that the other slower planets will be in different areas of the zodiac than the present-day. It is simply not possible to compare like with exact like. Yet this does not render the exercise futile. Noting those dates when Mars and Saturn are in conjunction (especially heliocentrically) can be thought of as a traffic signal. You are given warning of the impending need to stop or told to stop immediately. A review of these conjunctions shows that they often, like the Mars-Uranus aspects, mark a top from which the S&P especially falls for a few weeks.

For example: the last Aquarius conjunction of Mars-Saturn took place in 1990 when the S&P fell by five percent in the space of two weeks (a half lunar cycle). Their next heliocentric conjunction in this sign occurs on May 25, 2022.

That is followed by a Pisces conjunction on May 17, 2024. This conjunction is likely to be of especial importance as it coincides with the birthday of the NYSE. It may be that this marks the start of a decided move downward—quite in keeping with the information about both the Neptune and Pluto ingresses mentioned earlier in this work.

The Mars-Saturn Aries conjunction in May 2026 might be viewed as an inspection—a harbor master coming on board and checking the level of fuel in your tank, your general condition, and your plans. Indeed, we should all be ready for compulsory financial health checks in the second quarter of 2026.

Though trading techniques are not offered in this work, it is worth pointing out that when planets change signs at the same time as major aspects form (conjunctions especially), and perhaps within 24 hours of a New or Full Moon, there is usually a change of market direction. This is understandable as the clusters of activity have an effect on traders whose reaction to a change in the cosmic energy patterns prompts such markets moves. Indeed, an easy rule where markets are concerned is to note that when several planetary events takes place within a 48-hour period, change of trend is more likely than not. A few of these key dates are given in Appendix 12.

Mars aside, there is one other planet whose movements through the signs of the zodiac should be monitored as you move to "full speed ahead."

Jupiter

Jupiter takes 11.88 years to move through the signs, spending approximately one year in each. As Jupiter—the planet associated with optimism and expansion—moves through each sign, industries associated with that sign experience boom periods and related share-price rise. Note that this system does not take into account the chart of actual companies.

If you want to work with company charts—and this is a fabulous area to study—you will find that there are at least two charts for every company: its incorporation date, and any subsequent name change if applicable. The second is the date of its initial public offering (IPO). An experienced astro-trader will study these charts at length. Yet even knowing the sun-sign of the company's IPO is worthy of note. Comparing this position with Jupiter's position by sign will give clues as to whether or not this will be a buoyant year for the company or not.

If you have the full chart, then you can note which areas of the company chart will be impacted by Jupiter's sign change. This is a valuable exercise: it is in these areas that the company will want to expand and where costs could rise.

There is no short cut to financial success: research is always needed! Looking at a company chart should be thought of as detailed work. It is not always necessary if you are investing solely in market sectors or funds.

As with the other planets, Jupiter does not change sign on the same date each year, and spends rather longer in some signs than in others. At perihelion (near the Sun and in the signs of Pisces, Aries, and Taurus), Jupiter spends a relatively short, time compared to their opposite signs of Virgo, Libra and Scorpio. Where the time-frame is short it is vital to assess the impact of

Mars position alongside Jupiter. Promising aspects between these two planets will suggest dates when there might be a growth spurt manifesting in a boost to share price.

Also, in moving Full Steam Ahead, going with the current is obviously beneficial. By focusing on upcoming sectors as identified through Jupiter's position, the investor is doing precisely this: going with the flow. At the time of writing Jupiter is passing through Sagittarius, a sign it will visit again twelve years from now in 2031 to 2032. We can look at Jupiter's sojourn through each sign and identify which sectors are most likely to advance.

A little back-testing is useful. Jupiter moved through Scorpio – the sign associated with both oil and mining—between November 2017 and November 2018. The companies which clearly thrived as Jupiter transited this sign include Royal Dutch Shell (Oil), which saw revenue growth of 29.9%, Glencore (Mining) where revenue grew by eighteen percent and BP (oil and gas) with growth of over thirty percent.

Of course, the art is to buy into promising sectors ahead of Jupiter's arrival in a sign. Not to belabor the point: it would clearly be foolhardy to buy into just any company in the suggested sector. Instead, it is advisable, indeed essential, to look at the financial reports for each business before making investment. The advantage of using knowledge of Jupiter's position is that it reduces the numbers of companies you need to look at: directing you to those likely to see good progress. There are, after all, thousands and thousands of companies out there. Unless you are going to spread the risk by investing in a whole index, you do have to choose where to focus your investment energies.

Backdrop

No planet can be considered in isolation. And, as mentioned, Jupiter's move through any sign will be different from the last time it visited that particular area—as the other slow-moving planets will be in other zodiacal areas. Again, Jupiter's orbit is roughly 11.88 years. Pluto would probably have been in a different sign, as would Neptune and Uranus the last time that Jupiter passed through any sign. These three outer planets have a curious dance all of their own; but they have very definite impact on how different sectors will likely react to Jupiter's presence in a sign next time around.

In the next section, you will find the "Jupiter" areas to consider as you move ahead. The relevant dates are given below, and the likely impact that the three major ingresses of Neptune (to Aries in 2024), Pluto (to Aquarius in 2025), and Uranus (to Gemini in 2026) might have.

SAGITTARIUS (November 8, 2018–December 2, 2019

The two transits of Jupiter through Sagittarius considered here are very, very different. The first is set against the backdrop of Pluto in Capricorn, Neptune in Pisces, and Uranus in Taurus. The next transit, in the early 2030s, will have Pluto in Aquarius, Neptune in Aries, and Uranus by then moving into Cancer.

The sector most associated with Sagittarius is travel: the longer the journey the better. No two transits are identical however, and Jupiter's stay from late 2018 through late 2019 coincides with Neptune's transit of Pisces. The accent then is likely to be on travel "across oceans." It will likely also include those companies determined to "clean up" the oceans, removing accumulated waste (Pluto). While companies offering cruises could bring rewarding investment, it is should also be the case that those businesses offering clean fuel to ocean-going vessels will see their value increase. Attracting as much attention should be space travel and associated industries.

Sagittarius is said to be the great knowledge seeker, the ultimate pursuant of truth. Legal industries should do well through this period. So too should places of higher education. Yet we cannot—until Jupiter leaves this sign in 2019—rule out the possibility of publications and journalism being subjected to legal challenge, given Pluto's simultaneous presence in Capricorn.

The situation will be very different in the early 2030s. Jupiter will move through Sagittarius, Pluto will be in Aquarius, and Neptune in Aries. Indeed, there will be a time when the three planets are equidistant to one another—the implications being that they will be working in tandem. It is during this period that fast communications, international legal systems, and global learning (to include global university education) will surely take off. Indeed, given that Uranus (doing things differently) will be in home-loving Cancer, it may be that home schooling is the big winner. Thus, businesses offering the "best of the best" home teaching programs via the Internet will see exponential growth.

Of course education won't be the only area that develops rapidly under these conditions. There will be those who abhor the potential toxicity of wireless technology (Pluto in Aquarius), and who demand the legal rights (Jupiter in Sagittarius), to go off-grid (Uranus in Cancer). The back-drop of Neptune in Aries cannot be ignored either, with the high probability that many individuals will be demanding cleaner air. Thus, air purifying companies should do well especially if they can deliver warm air (Sagittarius is a fire sign) at speed (Aries = fast).

CAPRICORN (December 2, 2019–December 19, 2020)

This transit of Capricorn by Jupiter is interesting in that it coincides with both Saturn and Pluto moving through the same sign. Without the presence of these other two planets, we could reasonably draw the conclusion that Capricorn businesses and industries would experience Jupiterian expansion through this period.

Yet, Saturn acts as a regulator and Pluto stands for reinvention. We must then assume that only the fittest of these businesses will survive. It will, therefore, be even more important than usual to make background study of the health of these businesses before investing. Some, with inadequate capital base, will no doubt fail. Others, with a strong asset base, should exceed expectation and bring large bonuses to investors. Much will depend on how stable these institutions are before Jupiter arrives in this sign. Those businesses liable to fail may have expanded overseas (a common enough trend as Jupiter makes passage through Sagittarius), and reached further than their comfort zone or financial buffer can sustain. Changes in foreign currency exchange could also affect some of the businesses adversely. It is worth mentioning the strong possibility of trade wars scuppering many business plans through these years.

The Capricorn—usually corporate—businesses to consider investing in are those dealing with essentials: food and building particularly. Those working in the field of infrastructure might normally be deemed to benefit from this transit. Manufacturers providing materials—for building or clothing—would normally expect to see growth, especially where protective fabrics are concerned. Yet this transit coincides with the Lunar Node passing through Cancer (opposing Capricorn) and it may be that the money supply (limited by both Saturn and Pluto) dries up. Extraordinary care then would need to be taken before investing in these companies during this transit. It is vital that the health of the whole company be taken into account before investing.

Food and other essentials are different. There is always a demand for these. It will surely be vital to select for investment those companies able to withstand the pressure to provide better quality at better price as financial controls limit spending power.

On a positive note, Capricorn, the sign ruled by Saturn, aka "Old Father Time," is the sign associated with everything that calibrates time: watches and clocks. Companies (and dealers) working in these fields should experience expansion. Indeed, given that many people may be fearful of the future and experiencing the sense of having "no time to lose," it may be that the measurement of time is actually compelling to some investors. Those who feel that money isn't necessarily safe in the bank, may feel that they might as well wear a significant timepiece and pass this on to their heirs.

It has been mentioned that the bond market will likely collapse in the coming years. Through Jupiter's transit of Capricorn, this becomes even more possible. Jupiter has a justified reputation for exaggeration, and anything that has not been built on solid ground will doubtless collapse. Both government and corporate bonds may be unsafe.

In contrast, those businesses with sound wealth will likely

expand exponentially. It is true that some might justifiably be concerned about monopoly regulations being imposed upon them. Rumors of these will likely begin at the conjunction of Jupiter with Saturn in Aquarius in December 2020, and be heard loudly as Pluto crosses into that same sign in 2024. It will likely be important that these companies are seen to plow a proportion of profits back into the communities where aid is most needed. Indeed, by 2024, the days of excessive bonuses being awarded to CEOs will be over.

AQUARIUS (December 19, 2020–May 13, 2021 and July 28, 2021–December 29, 2021)

Again, this particular transit by Jupiter is unusual in that Saturn, too, will be moving through Aquarius: marking the start of a fresh business cycle. This increases the likelihood of companies associated with this sign exceeding expectation. Jupiter is thought of as expansive and Saturn quite the opposite. In business terms, the two counterbalance one another—so that moves forward are underpinned by careful thought and secure capitalization.

With their conjunction in Aquarius, we should assume that it will be the high-tech industries that see fast growth with matching returns. It would not be surprising if the space industry (and possibly a race into space) becomes apparent through these months. Aquarius is one of the Air signs. It is noted for futuristic tendencies (hence the potential for the space industry to develop at speed through this period). Yet terrestrial activity should be assessed: aviation including helicopter and drone manufacturing should fare well.

The computing industry might also be considered a promising investment area. Saturn's presence here could result in a curious twist. It has become the norm to think of computers and associated equipment becoming smaller and easier to carry, but having the capability to hold multiple and useful apps. Saturn's presence in Aquarius suggests that there might be a return to those slightly larger models that act as phone first and internet second. Aging populations may well have a preference for those instruments which do all that they need them to do without all the extras.

Note that the two periods listed are separated by a matter of weeks—when Jupiter moves through Aquarius. In the second of these periods, Jupiter's revisit of Aquarius covers a few weeks when Jupiter is retrograde. It is entirely possible that those companies showing promise during the first Jupiter in Aquarius period will NOT do well through this second period. However, if share prices in related industries rose during the first period, this second period offers a buying opportunity.

PISCES (May 13, 2021–July 28, 2021, December 29, 2021– May 10, 2022, and October 2022–December 20, 2022)

Between May 2021 and the December 2022 solstice, Jupiter moves into Pisces, retrogrades back into Aquarius, returns to Pisces, moves on into Aries, and then crosses back into Pisces. This is not unusual: it relates to Jupiter's orbital position relative to the Sun. It does, however, suggest that the period from May 2021 to December 2022 will see sectors vying with one another to be "lead sectors." As before, the retrograde periods offer buying opportunities.

Pisces must surely be the "Internet" sign. Like water (Pisces) the internet is everywhere. It has no respect for legal borders and has been used by those who wish to circumvent the law. Many believe it should be dismantled completely and then reconstructed. If such a task were to be undertaken, then this eighteen month period might be deemed the optimum time to undertake the task. Jupiter's association with the law, and the high probability given the position of the slow-moving planets, is that governments will seek to place curbs on its use—perhaps as part of a global plan. Certainly, through this period, developments in this area should defy all present expectation. Identifying those companies involved in the process should be possible during Jupiter's second transit of Aquarius BETWEEN July 28 and December 29, 2021.

Pisces is also the sign most connected with the sea and fishing. Firms operating in this area—together with ocean carriers (cruise and container ships) should witness a boom period. Also to be considered are those companies focused on foot health and footwear.

Developments in medicine—especially bio-energetics should be marked. With considerable accent on mental health and better understanding of the brain as center of the nervous system, new attitudes to mental health and different types of care should emerge. Spas and sanctuaries should see growth.

Taking into account Pluto's presence in Capricorn as Jupiter moves through the last quarter of the zodiac (2019–2022), care of the elderly—specifically those over 84 years of age, should also result in growth in the number of service companies offering care for this age group. As always, the fundamentals of the company and its chart need to be carefully studied before investing.

ARIES (May 10, 2022–October 28, 2022 and December 20, 2022–May 16, 2023)

Aries stocks cover anything linked with fire and energy—and yes, that includes military hardware. Aries, ruled by Mars, also covers anything sharp: so companies using hard metals to produce cutting (surgical) tools are included in this group. Recalling that the effect of Pluto's transit through Capricorn has coincided with the disintegration of much infrastructure, it's probable that there will be growing demand for metal and other "hard" materials necessary to replace these. Jupiter's transit of this sign coincides with the expected low in the business cycle, so that growth in this sector may not be as great as it was when Jupiter last visited this area of the zodiac in 2012. That said, given the high probability of escalating tensions threatening war in many areas of the world, those companies servicing the army, navy and air forces of many countries will surely be ready clients—prompting profit and growth in the military-industrial complex.

Aries is also the sign of the pioneer and explorer. Firms offering mountaineering and orienteering products should fare well.

As an aside, and following on from some recent and fascinating discussion with a client, those deciding to live "off the grid" in their retirement are now making significant purchases in the items needed for this way of life. They are likely buying at the right time—i.e., before prices for these items rise during 2022.

Copper is generally associated with Venus-ruled Taurus and it is to be expected that the price of this commodity will rise as Jupiter moves through Taurus in 2023. As Jupiter moves through Aries, however, companies using copper in their products should find that the price is acceptable and that they can therefore make products at reasonable prices. This, together with increased demand, should ensure that these businesses thrive, offering, a year later, healthy return to their investors.

It should be remembered that as Jupiter transits Aries, Neptune will be moving toward that sign. By this stage, a new space race may well be underway—with this sector promising much and share prices in businesses supplying essentials in this area soaring as a result. To be clear however; though these prices will likely move quickly in an upwardly trajectory, they could fall just as quickly when Jupiter reaches Taurus in May 2023. If choosing to purchase shares in this sector, it might be wise to consider buying in 2022 but, unless wholly confident in the fundamentals of a company, sell these shares by May 2023.

TAURUS (May 16, 2023–May 25, 2024)

Recall that this transit coincides with a period when more than one of the slower-moving planets moves from one sign of the zodiac to another: Jupiter moves through Taurus as Pluto prepares to leave Capricorn. This emphasis on Earth signs will likely also coincide with increased demand for physical wealth: as in coins, gold, silver, platinum etc. The price of copper is also likely to increase however, resulting in the firms that did well a year earlier, finding that costs are rising and that they need to raise prices: at which point demand will surely fall.

It is probable that those still in a position to make purchases will be drawn to quality items built to last. A move away from throwaway clothes, and toward durability and high quality should result in demand for better fabrics and sustainable items of all kinds. The price of these goods is set to rise along with the profit of those businesses providing such goods.

Taurus is ruled by Venus, which is associated with sugar. It is reasonable to conclude that confectioners will do well in Jupiter's Taurus year. So too should those food retailers supplying "comfort foods." Selecting for investment companies and businesses supplying organic, natural, and free-from-pesticide products should result in good returns.

There is a school of thought suggesting that Taurus is ruled by Earth rather than Venus. Certainly those born under this sign seem to have deep appreciation for natural and "earthy" products (as well as enjoying good food and wines). Taking Neptune's position by sign into consideration, we might by this time be much more aware of the value of nutrition—prompting ever-increasing demand for organic foods. Since these, by definition, require optimum growing conditions—and that the solar activity of this period may not be optimum—a shortage of these goods should see prices rise as a result of increased demand and limited supply.

Ahead of Jupiter's arrival might be considered an optimum period to invest in "smart farming." Developments in this area since Jupiter's arrival in Capricorn (another Earth sign) are likely to have been considerable.

It has been noted through previous Jupiter in Taurus periods that there is increased demand for leather goods (especially when used for furniture). Taking into account the position of Saturn, Uranus, Neptune, and Pluto, the demand for quality—and likely large—pieces of luggage should increase.

GEMINI (May 25, 2024–June 9, 2025)

The outer planets, Pluto and Neptune move into new signs as Jupiter passes through Gemini. This is when the financial waves will likely be most turbulent, the seas rougher, and when many of our financial ships could run aground.

Determining what will drive these problems is not easy. Yet

a strong possibility is that the impact of artificial intelligence, block-chain technology, and crypto-currencies will be felt acutely. Though likely in wide use by then, even these could be subject to disruption by solar activity. Fail-safes will need to be in place. Companies that can provide any extra security (back-up services) will doubtless be able to charge large amounts for their services. Yet, of course, if there is no crisis and their services not needed, then this investment might not pay magical dividends! This is where risk assessment needs to be undertaken and where both the company and the individual's chart must be considered.

Artificial Intelligence is already an area of rapid growth. Covering everything from intelligent refrigerators and other home products to transport and smart farming, AI is clearly the future. By 2024 demand for these products and services will likely be beyond anything we can so far imagine. Resistance to their development will be futile: so it may be preferable to invest in this fast-growing area rather than do the ostrich thing of burying our investment heads in the sand.

Robotics too should be considered as belonging to the Gemini sector. Growth in this area is likely to be exponential as Jupiter passes through this sign. Since deliveries and postal services come under the Gemini heading as well, it's probable that this will be the year when drone deliveries become regular features of our skies. Firms using robots to create packaging should also offer investment potential.

Away from this type of technology—but still offering their own high-tech versions—those businesses offering short distance transport (and yes, that includes bicycles and self-driven vehicles) should also see growth.

These various products will require developers with special skills. Again those who have mastered more than one computing language, and who can build networks crossing from one type of system to another, will surely be in great demand. Either acquiring these skills or investing in those honing this ability, and launching enterprises offering this service should be considered in the years prior to Jupiter's arrival in this area. You might want to take advantage of the surge in demand—and therefore hopefully in profits—in this sector.

Communication services cover a wide range of products including the mastery of foreign language: this ability will also be much in demand—especially those who can cross from Western to Eastern languages.

CANCER (June 9, 2025–June 30, 2026)

It is "usual" for companies providing essential—very often home-building and home-making services—to experience growth as Jupiter moves through Cancer. Though this may well be true again in 2025 and 2026, it is against the background of recession and perhaps war.

Cancer craves security, and perhaps because of the threat of war or concern about limited supplies, and even, perhaps, broken supply chains, security will be on the minds of many. Businesses offering related services and products will doubtless experience growth.

If history repeats itself, then the safe, war-free areas of the world should also see expansion in their hospitality industries. While global hotel chains will likely suffer if long distance travel becomes difficult, those offering more locally based price breaks should do well.

Cancer might be described as the "bread-basket" of the zodiac. At a literal level then, bakeries ought to flourish. Yet so too should all food suppliers, laundries, kitchenware, and home management services—though shortages and distribution difficulties will no doubt cause ripples of anxiety for management.

The boating industry should also thrive as Jupiter passes through Cancer as should those companies offering navigation equipment.

Cancer is ruled by the Moon which is sometimes described as "silvery." Silver goods and companies specializing in the use of silver, ought to thrive through the period too.

Under "normal" Jupiter rules, an increase in the value of real estate would be obvious as Jupiter moved through Cancer. There may well be a flurry of activity as Jupiter passes through Cancer's first few degrees. However, taking into account the nodal position—and the high probability of global recession—this is unlikely to be the case. Those with cash should, however, find that there are many properties for sale from which they could receive rental income.

LEO (June 30, 2026–July 26, 2027)

Whereas Cancer is focused on security and home comfort, Leo reaches out to embrace fun and enjoyment. The contrast between the two can also be seen in the way in which gains are made in sectors associated with each sign. In a Jupiter in Cancer year, money is spent on improving homes. With Jupiter in Leo the accent shifts to pleasure—hobbies and leisure activities.

That is certainly what happened when Jupiter passed through Leo during the twentieth century. Its transit through Leo from mid-2026 to mid-2027 is likely, however, to be very different indeed.

Recall that this transit coincides with Pluto moving through Leo's opposite sign Aquarius. On July 20, 2026, the first Jupiter-Pluto opposition in these signs for over two centuries will occur. Thanks to retrograde periods, there will be three more across the Leo-Aquarius axis in 2039. It is interesting to note that the last time this aspect—across the zodiacal axis—took place was September 2, 1789. On that VERY DATE, the US Treasury Department was established by Congress.

The fact that such a step was necessary says something about the challenges that led to this decision. Ten days later, Alexander Hamilton was appointed First Secretary of the Treasury, and just a week later negotiated loans from New York City banks.

The Jupiter-Pluto cycle has a justified reputation for being the "wealth cycle." Their opposition can be a signal for impending bankruptcy. It is entirely possible that within days of July 26, 2026, the USA will once again require financial help to continue to pay its administration. This could be a bleak time for the nation.

With that being the case, hobbies and leisure activity might not be uppermost in the minds of many people.

Nor will the Unites States will be the only nation facing

crippling debt through this period. The disparity between the "haves and the have-nots" may well lead to difficulties elsewhere. It should be recalled that the French revolution took place in 1789!

The likelihood of July 2027 being an important period in world history increases when we observe that Jupiter and Pluto oppose one another at 4° degrees of that axis. The same day, Neptune is at 4° Aries, while Uranus is at 4° Gemini: putting Neptune on the exact midpoint of Uranus and Pluto.

The Uranus-Pluto cycle is recognized as bringing upheaval, while Neptune's presence here indicates that any upheaval will be widespread and all-encompassing. Development at this scale will surely be overwhelming for many who attempt to hold on to past structures. They may eschew what they view as technologies gone mad and try instead to revert to old bartering systems.

While the demand for some products and services that might have been expected to be rise during this period may be reduced, it could also be that the trade in jewelry and precious metals increases.

Of course it is possible that the demand for theatrical performance as a form of escapism will also lead to a rise in the share price of many of the big players in this field. Given that in the past, the presence of Jupiter in Leo has also led to a desire for dressing fabulously, those businesses providing costume services (including uniforms and accessories) will likely see increased demand and consequent rise in their share price. The fashion industry too should be considered for investment as the demand for designer clothes and accessories will likely be high.

It is not abnormal to see a spike in luxury hotel profits as Jupiter moves through Leo— though this will be much dependent on exactly were in the world these are based. As outlined earlier, war is a distinct possibility for this period.

Whatever the constraints experienced by governments— and if past behavior does indeed offer a clue to the future—the gambling industry should do well. Casinos, and those providing the equipment for these, should see burgeoning growth during these years. It is doubtful that this will be achieved through mainstream investment. Gambling might even be prohibited—

presumably in an attempt by governments to see transparency in financial transactions and to collect essential taxes. This though could drive this behavior into a black market economy where winnings may be huge.

VIRGO (July 26, 2027–August 2028)

First, note that as Jupiter reaches this sign, the Lunar Node starts its journey through the upswing of the business cycle. This is when recovery should begin. It will perhaps be unsurprising that Virgo-style companies take the lead. Associated industries include everything to do with day-to-day essentials, data management, and health. Cleaning up and clearing-up products are also considered to be Virgo industries.

Noting the presence of Uranus in Gemini, Neptune in Aries, and Pluto in Aquarius by this time, the industries that should take off at speed will surely be those using the most up-to-date of technologies and those which will be fighting pollution. Anticipate fast-paced developments in this area as Jupiter moves through Virgo. But also remember that it will form a square to Uranus. As the faster moving of the two, Jupiter reaches this—its first quarter phase with Uranus—in September 2027. This marks the first "staging" post of the cycle which began in 2024. It is entirely possible that ideas which have been incubating between 2024 and 2027 will—quite suddenly—have widespread appeal, bringing profit to those investors who made early forays into this sector.

Developments in manufacturing—presumably of robots— for this new age should expand. The interesting thing here is that though the costs of building these may be high as Pluto journeys through Capricorn, from 2024, these costs are likely to fall substantially. Assuming that there are no difficulties with distribution (requiring satellites to be undamaged by solar interference), then with the costs of these products falling as demand increases, this area should prove to be a profitable area for investment.

Health industries too should offer promising rewards by the

end of this period. Generally it is best to buy into a promising sector while Jupiter passes through the sign earlier. It may not be too late, even in early July 2027, to buy in at good prices. Don't omit those industries that provide essential cleaning equipment. They should do exceptionally well.

So too might those companies offering therapeutic care to those who have suffered mental illness in the previous years. New drugs will be coming on to the market. But, by the time that both Uranus and Pluto reach Air signs in 2025, growing acknowledgement of the benefit of talking therapies and sanctuaries offering respite and care to those who suffer should flourish.

LIBRA (August 24, 2028 – September 24, 2029)

The sign of Libra is depicted as a set of scales: sometimes balanced and sometimes not. When Jupiter moves through this sign legal affairs tend to dominate the news. Published articles bring advertising opportunities. Expansion in the number of takeovers or mergers—whether hostile or friendly, requires the expertise of contract lawyers. It is not at all unusual for legal firms to expand during Jupiter's visit to this sign.

Given that both Uranus and Pluto will be moving through Air signs simultaneously, we should also expect that the number of patents applied for will increase exponentially—again adding to the legal workload, but also to the profitability of firms working in this sector.

Venus-ruled Libra is also associated with the beauty industry. Here again the share prices of cosmetic companies and, to a degree, some pharmaceutical companies will likely also surge.

Fashion houses too should see burgeoning interest in their products with fabric manufacturers and those with skills in lace and embroidery, and, of course, designing doing well.

Firms specializing in architecture: building (bridges especially), website design, and in creating machines whose elegance and efficiency brings them notice, should also experience increased interest in their products and service with consequent rise in their share price.

Given the accent on Air signs coupled with Neptune's transit of Aries, we should also expect to see growth in the space race, in rockets, and all the items needed to make these successful, as well as new forms of air transport.

Another area for the would-be investor to consider would be in those companies specializing in weather forecasting. Demand for these services and for ever-more accurate GPS systems should see this sector grow.

SCORPIO (September 24, 2029 – October 22, 2030)

This sector won't be for everyone, but there is a connection between Scorpio and the military. There is also a connection with the finance industry, particularly lending to large businesses. Despite gathering clouds on some financial horizons, high-end luxury goods should also see growth. Also to be considered are industries involved in waste disposal and in clean up. Here the growth in "ocean cleaning" should be exponential. Data-mining is also a sector to be considered. Tempting as it may be to consider mining generally, note that over the previous three cycles, the immediate effect of Jupiter's arrival in Scorpio has seen a pullback in these shares—at least as Jupiter travels through the first few degrees of the sign. This though could be the optimum time to buy in.

It is through this last year of the 2020s decade that those born with Pluto in Scorpio, who invested in bio-research, could reap rich reward. Again, we must assume that they will have studied the company's fundamentals. This though is the year when success and reward are most likely.

We should also expect, as between late 2017 and November 2018, that oil and mining companies will exceed market expectation.

Dear Readers,

Though some people are born into wealth and face different challenges than the majority, most of us have been faced with turbulent financial seas. It is a valuable exercise to think back to how you coped and what steps got you to where you are today. Recognizing ebb and flow is a first step in accepting the presence of financial tides and then riding them.

It could be argued that the art of living is accommodating to these rhythms. No situation is ever permanent. Most of us cling to the past, and rather too many people reaching retirement age today have been indoctrinated with the idea that we can and should learn from history. It is implied that we should not repeat what have since been deemed errors or mistakes. Our judgment is said to be improved by understanding earlier endeavors. Though this argument is understandable, dwelling on the past can detract us from looking forward. In the knowledge that a new tide will appear on the horizon, we are well placed to prepare for the future and the opportunities this brings.

Though I am of the opinion that close scrutiny of planetary cycles—their waxing and waning—is of value in determining probable future trends, I am also aware that any statements made are a blend of that scrutiny and imagination. Cycles never repeat exactly.

For example, we may say that "the last time Uranus and Pluto were in square (right angle to one another) such and such occurred, and therefore a variation on that theme is probable the next time they form this angle." The fact is, however, that other planets will be situated at new points in the zodiac. It is not possible to match exactly the cosmic patterns or planetary pictures with another time in recorded history.

Research is fascinating and through it, it is possible for me to hazard an opinion as to the probable effect of various planetary/ astrological configurations. Over time however, that opinion, based on likelihood and imagination alters: sometimes subtly and at other times dramatically.

Some of you will know that I publish a free monthly newsletter. This letter was originally sent out weekly in 1996, to just eight clients. In the last twelve years, the format and frequency have changed. The Full Moon letter has been issued monthly since 2006 and has a readership of several thousand. These missives afford the opportunity to make up-to-date comment on economic, social, and political trends, as well occasionally signaling promising investment dates and sectors. If you aren't on our regular mailing list, you can sign up for it via www.financialuniverse.co.uk

Of necessity, the focus of this book has been general. Yet you will be navigating your own financial journey. You might compare notes with others but, essentially, you have to captain your own ship – though hopefully, a harbor master will be available to guide you from time to time.

Even if you are an experienced astrologer (perhaps even a master of planet cycles), you will benefit from learning more from those who monitor other recognized cycles (e.g. weather) and from discussing strategies with a financial advisor. Other readers, not skilled in planet-watching, may be experienced technical analysts or fund managers intrigued by the possibility of planetary cycles lending additional and useful information to their financial forecasting. Still others may be enthusiastic to assess their planetary rhythms as revealed through their birth chart. Everyone will surely benefit from meeting with others with similar interests.

* * *

Although there is considerable material now available on the world-wide web, there is perhaps no substitute from attending conferences, listening to researchers and making friends with like-minded individuals.

Here is a list of useful web addresses.

www.alexandriaibase.org
www.astrologicalassociation.com
www.astrology.org.uk
www.astrosoftware.com
www.financialuniverse.co.uk
www.geocosmic.org
www.keplercollege.org
www.uraniatrust.org

I am pleased to announce too, that in response to the many requests following earlier books, that a financial course will be launched at the Full Moon on September 14, 2019. Details of this can also be found at www.financialuniverse.co.uk

Navigating the Financial Universe has been an important work for me. Though there is much yet for me to learn, in preparing each chapter, I have had recourse to the many astro-financial journeys of clients, and enjoyed daily confirmation that there really is correlation between planetary cycle and financial affairs.

It is quite clear that the planetary gear changes of the coming decade will afford some extra-ordinary opportunities. I hope that the hints given in this work and subsequently bolstered in the Full Moon monthly letter will be of assistance in your financial journey.

Yours from the stars

Christeen

APPENDICES

Planetary Conjunctions
with the Galactic Center 2019–2029

Jupiter	November 14, 2019
Mars	February 10, 2020
Mars	January 19, 2022
Mars	December 30, 2023
Mars	December 10, 2025
Mars	November 20, 2027
Mars	October 29, 2029

Pluto Sign Changes 1930–2030

Geocentric Positions

Leo	October 7, 1937 to November 25, 1937
Cancer	November 25, 1937 to August 3, 1938
Leo	August 3, 1938 to February 7, 1939
Cancer	February 7, 1939 to June 14, 1939
Leo	June 14, 1939 to October 20, 1956
Virgo	October 20, 1956 to January 15, 1957
Leo	January 15, 1957 to August 19, 1957
Virgo	August 19, 1957 to April 11, 1958
Leo	April 11, 1958 to June 10, 1958
Virgo	June 10, 1958 to October 5, 1971
Libra	October 5, 1971 to April 17, 1972
Virgo	April 17, 1972 to July 30, 1972
Libra	July 30, 1972 to November 5, 1983
Scorpio	November 5, 1983 to May 18, 1984
Libra	May 18, 1984 to August 28, 1984
Scorpio	August 28, 1984 to January 17, 1995
Sagittarius	January 17, 1995 to April 21, 1995

Scorpio	April 21, 1995 to November 10, 1995
Sagittarius	November 10, 1995 to January 26, 2008
Capricorn	January 26, 2008 to June 14, 2008
Sagittarius	June 14, 2008 to November 27, 2008
Capricorn	November 27, 2008 to March 23, 2023
Aquarius	March 23, 2023 to June 11, 2023
Capricorn	June 11, 2023 to January 21, 2024
Aquarius	January 21, 2024 to September 2, 2024
Capricorn	September 2, 2024 to November 19, 2024
Aquarius	November 19, 2024 to March 9, 2043

Notes on Moon Signs

ARIES: Potentially an impulse shopper. Cash flows fast. Needs to see quick gains in investments. Rarely undertakes risk management but has the courage to back a hunch. If things don't work out and losses are incurred, hard feelings are rare: this group move swiftly on to the next thing.

TAURUS: Shrewd shoppers. Willing to wait—or haggle—to get a good price Drawn to quality but rarely pays full price. Goes for long-term investments often in the form of jewelry and shows preference for investing in longstanding companies paying good dividends.

GEMINI: Often have great investment ideas but rarely follow these through, as they are so easily distracted. Not the best of shoppers either! Rarely keeps to a plan or list. Attracted to fund investments covering a variety of fields and interests.

CANCER: The hoarders and collectors. This group spends more than most on their homes. Though they will complain about not having enough savings, they usually arrange something to "fall back on." Superb at husbanding resources.

LEO: Determination to get what they want and when they want it can lead this group to spending more than is necessary: though with age they learn to control these urges. They often master the fine art of timing too, and can be superb technical analysts, resulting in developing sound buy-sell strategies.

VIRGO: Though avid readers of financial papers, these individuals can be super fretful. The ups and down, gains and losses, can be deeply unsettling. True, they tend not to shop (for items or investments) until they've undertaken much research. It also seems true that they can miss the investment boat by selling too early or buying too late. They are best suited to long-term investment.

LIBRA: Apparently naturally indecisive. Wants to know what YOU think before acting. Yet can also be a risk taker. Slow to quit while ahead. Though genuinely believes that the sales will right themselves. Too easily seduced into buying—and so experiences expensive financial mistakes.

SCORPIO: Cash doesn't leave this wallet easily. This group will save for what they want—or do without altogether. Often misses the financial boat as they await a "better" moment to buy. Yet are often fabulous sellers—knowing exactly when to make best gains.

SAGITTARIUS: Easy come and easy go. Cash flow is usually fast and furious. Attracted to foreign investment (often in the form of an adventure or holiday!). Confident spender with a knack of buying when prices represent good value. Not natural savers.

CAPRICORN: Cautious spenders. Masters of timing in both spending and purchasing. Conscious of value and willing to pay for the best. Good long-term investors. Can also make good day traders if given sufficient time and space to study trends.

AQUARIUS: Absolutely does not respond well to the hard sell. Needs to arrive at their own conclusion about value and price. An eccentric attitude to finance doesn't endear them to financial advisors! Develops a quirky investment portfolio and can build/hoard savings.

PISCES: There are two types here. One can be dreamy, idealistic and unclear about money matters. The other can go completely the other way and be the finest book-keeper imaginable. Either way there is the feeling that everything "ought" to be perfect. What both types have in common is inattention to long-term savings. Both also benefit from having partners or advisors assisting with their long-term planning.

Jupiter Ingress (Geocentric)

Capricorn	December 2, 2019 to December 19, 2020
Aquarius	December 19, 2020 to May 13, 2021
Pisces	May 13, 2021 to July 28, 2021
Aquarius	July 28, 2021 to December 29, 2021
Pisces	December 29, 2021 to May 10, 2022
Aries	May 10, 2022 to October 28, 2022
Pisces	October 28, 2022 to December 20, 2022
Aries	December 20, 2022 to May 16, 2023
Taurus	May 16, 2023 to May 25, 2024
Gemini	May 25, 2024 to June 9, 2025
Cancer	June 9, 2025 to June 30, 2026
Leo	June 30, 2026 to July 26, 2027
Virgo	July 26, 2027 to August 24, 2028
Libra	August 24, 2028 to September 24, 2029
Scorpio	September 24, 2029 to October 22, 2030
Sagittarius	October 22, 2030 to November 15, 2031

Mercury Geocentric Stations 2019-2030

R = Retrograde D = Direct
Dynamic Report

July 8, 2019	04° Leo 27'	R
August 1, 2019	23° Cancer 56'	D
October 31, 2019	27° Scorpio 38'	R
November 20, 2019	11° Scorpio 35'	D
February 17, 2020	12° Pisces 53'	R
March 10, 2020	28° Aquarius 12'	D
June 18, 2020	14° Cancer 45'	R
July 12, 2020	05° Cancer 09'	D
October 14, 2020	11° Scorpio 40'	R
November 3, 2020	25° Libra 53'	D
January 30 2021	26° Aquarius 29'	R
February 21, 2021	11° Aquarius 01'	D
May 29, 2021	24° Gemini 43'	R
June 22, 2021	16° Gemini 07'	D
September 27, 2021	25° Libra 28'	R
October 18, 2021	10° Libra 07'	D

204   Navigating the Financial Universe

January 14, 2022	10°Aquarius 20'	R
February 4, 2022	24°Capricorn 22'	D
May 10, 2022	04°Gemini 51'	R
June 3, 2022	26°Taurus 05'	D
September 10, 2022	08°Libra 55'	R
October 2, 2022	24°Virgo 11'	D
December 29, 2022	24°Capricorn 21'	R
January 18, 2023	08°Capricorn 08'	D
April 21, 2023	15°Taurus 37'	R
May 15, 2023	05°Taurus 50'	D
August 23, 2023	21°Virgo 51'	R
September 15, 2023	08°Virgo 00'	D
December 13, 2023	08°Capricorn 09'	R
January 2, 2024	22°Sagittarius 10'	D
April 1, 2024	27°Aries 13'	R
April 25, 2024	15°Aries 58'	D
August 5, 2024	04°Virgo 06'	R
August 28, 2024	21°Leo 24'	D
November 26, 2024	22°Sagittarius 40'	R
December 15, 2024	06°Sagittarius 23'	D

March 15, 2025	09°Aries 35'	R
April 7, 2025	26°Pisces 49'	D
July 18, 2025	15°Leo 34'	R
August 11, 2025	04°Leo 14'	D
November 9, 2025	06°Sagittarius 51'	R
November 29, 2025	20°Scorpio 42'	D
February 26, 2026	22°Pisces 33'	R
March 20, 2026	08°Pisces 29'	D
June 29, 2026	26°Cancer 15'	R
July 23, 2026	16°Cancer 18'	D
October 24, 2026	20°Scorpio 58'	R
November 13, 2026	05°Scorpio 02'	D
February 9, 2027	05°Pisces 58'	R
March 3, 2027	20°Aquarius 55'	D
June 10, 2027	06°Cancer 21'	R
July 4, 2027	27°Gemini 28'	D
October 7, 2027	04°Scorpio 55'	R
October 28, 2027	19°Libra 18'	D
January 24, 2028	19°Aquarius 41'	R
February 14, 2028	03°Aquarius 59'	D

May 21, 2028	16°Gemini18'	R
June 14, 2028	07°Gemini45'	D
September 19, 2028	18°Libra35'	R
October 11, 2028	03°Libra28'	D
January 7, 2029	03°Aquarius38'	R
January 27, 2029	17°Capricorn32'	D
May 1, 2029	26°Taurus40'	R
May 25, 2029	17°Taurus33'	D
September 2, 2029	01°Libra49'	R
September 25, 2029	17°Virgo26'	D
December 22, 2029	17°Capricorn42'	R
January 11, 2030	01°Capricorn26'	D
April 13, 2030	07°Taurus47'	R
May 6, 2030	27°Aries26'	D
August 16, 2030	14°Virgo29'	R
September 8, 2030	01°Virgo06'	D
December 6, 2030	01°Capricorn51'	R
December 25, 2030	15°Sagiattrius33'	D

Saturn Geocentric Ingress Dates

(Please note some of these occur as Saturn is retrograde (R)

March 22, 2020	Aquarius	D
July 2, 2020	Capricorn	R
December 17, 2020	Aquarius	D
March 7, 2023	Pisces	D
March 23, 2023	Aquarius	D
June 11, 2023	Capricorn	R
January 21, 2024	Aquarius	D
September 2, 2024	Capricorn	R
November 19, 2024	Aquarius	D
May 25, 2025	Aries	D
September 1, 2025	Pisces	D
February 14, 2026	Aries	D
April 13, 2028	Taurus	D
June 1, 2030	Gemini	D
July 14, 2032	Cancer	D

APPENDIX 7

Mars Conjunct Jupiter (Geocentric)

March 20, 2020

May 29, 2022

August 14, 2024

November 16, 2026

July 19, 2029

September 28, 2031

December 1, 2033

APPENDIX 8

Sun Conjunct Jupiter

December 27, 2019

January 29, 2021

March 5, 2022

April 11, 2023

May 18, 2024

June 24, 2025

July 29, 2026

August 31, 2027

September 30, 2028

October 30, 2029

November 30, 2030

January 1, 2032

February 2, 2033

March 10, 2034

APPENDIX 9

Mars stations

September 9, 2020	R	28°Aries 08'
November 14, 2020	D	15°Aries 13'
October 30, 2022	R	25°Gemini 36'
January 12, 2023	D	08°Gemini 07'
December 6, 2024	R	06°Leo 10'
February 24, 2025	D	17°Cancer 00'
January 10, 2027	R	10°Virgo 25'
April 1, 2027	D	20°Leo 55'
February 14, 2029	R	13°Libra 55'
May 5, 2029	D	24°Virgo 55'
March 29, 2031	R	21°Scorpio 38'
June 13, 2031	D	04°Scorpio 26'

Mars Out-of-Bounds

(with declination over 23 degrees and 27 minutes either North or South)

April 20, 2019 to June 12, 2019

February 9, 2020 to March 2, 2020

March 21, 2021 to May 24, 2021

January 12, 2022 to February 10, 2022

October 22, 2022 to May 4, 2023

December 20, 2023 to January 23, 2024

September 7, 2024 to September 17, 2024

December 30, 2024 to April 7, 2025

November 27, 2025 to January 4, 2026

August 3, 2026 to August 28, 2026

November 5, 2027 to December 17, 2027

July 7, 2028 to August 9, 2028

October 9, 2029 to November 28, 2029

Mars conjunct or opposing Uranus (Geocentric)

February 13, 2019	Conjunction	29°Aries 11'
November 24, 2019	Opposition	03°Scorpio 32'
January 20, 2021	Conjunction	06°Taurus 44'
November 17, 2021	Opposition	12°Scorpio 15'
August 1, 2022	Conjunction	18°Taurus 42'
November 11, 2023	Opposition	21°Scorpio 08'
July 15, 2024	Conjunction	26°Taurus 19'
November 4, 2025	Opposition	00°Sagittarius 08'
July 4, 2026	Conjunction	03°Gemini 52'
October 28, 2027	Opposition	09°Sagittarius
June 23, 2028	Conjunction	11°Gemini 24'
October 19, 2029	Opposition	18°Sagittarius 16'
June 15, 2030	Conjunction	19°Gemini 01'
October 6, 2031	Opposition	27°Sagittarius 15'

Appendix 12

Cluster Dates

Please note that these are just a selection of dates when market activity is likely to be above average. More comprehensive detail is given in the free Full Moon newsletter available via: *www.financialuniverse.co.uk*

2020: January 11–13 and September 7–9

2021: January 4, April 20–25, October 7–9, and November 10–16

2022: March 6–8, April 2, May 7–11, October 29–November 4

2023: March 15–18, May 17–28, June 30, and October 21–November 4

2024: May 17–28 (echoing the previous year), August 14–22, November 17–19

2025: January 20, March 12–17, April 20 and 21, May 30–June 2, October 10–15

2026: January 12–17, April 24–26, July 21–26 and November 15–18

2027: February 17–19, May 25–29, October 6–10 and November 12–15

2028 January 4–11, April 28–May 3, June 14–20, August 2 and November 21–25

2029: January 15–17, March 17–20, April 29–May 2, October 29–November 4

Index

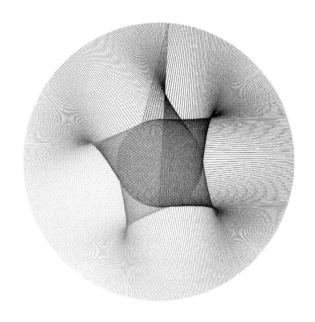

A Note on the Back Cover Image

This image with the 5 points displays the heliocentric positions of Saturn and Neptune in rectangular coordinates calculated every 100 days. There are 598 calculations (in other words, calculated on 598 days. And because they are done every 100 days, this covers a time span of 59,800 days).

Because Saturn and Neptune move slowly calculating every 100 days gives enough time for some noticeable separation between the planets.

The mandala is created by drawing a line between the positions of Saturn and Neptune on a particular day and then moving forward in time some number of days and drawing a line between the planets again. These mandalas are for the planets Saturn and Neptune.

This image is created with the Sirius 3.0 software, which is a very flexible and powerful astrology software available from Cosmic Patterns Software at www.AstroSoftware.com.

Acknowledgements

Navigating the Financial Universe was written for the readers of my regular monthly newsletter. Thanks are due to those who have been reading those missives for the last decade and whose occasional, but regular, enquiries and responses left me aware of their interest in my view of the future. *Navigating* was written for you.

From early discussions about this work over a wonderful lunch in Florida, Yvonne Paglia, the publisher, was behind the project giving gentle advice and asking thought-provoking questions. I owe much gratitude to Yvonne for her unequivocal support.

The book's title was determined by my husband who understood exactly what I wanted to achieve in writing it, and who supported its incubation without reading a single word of it. I hope one day that he will read a few chapters and find it useful!

Every single word has been read by the finest editor and supporter I could possibly ask for. James Wasserman gave me every encouragement from early draft to final production. As with *Exploring the Financial Universe* and *The Beginner's Guide to the Financial Universe*, the final production is down to his genius.

About the Author

CHRISTEEN H. SKINNER is the author of the best selling books from Ibis Press *Exploring the Financial Universe* and *Beginner's Guide to the Finacial Universe,* as well as *Money Signs* and *The Financial Universe.* She is a practicing astrologer based in London, with clients all over the world. She works with entrepreneurs and traders and is Director of Cityscopes London, a company specializing in future casting. She holds a Diploma from the Faculty of Astrological Studies where she taught for a decade. She has been Chair of the Astrological Association of Great Britain, Chair of the Advisory Board of National Council for Geocosmic Research, and is a Trustee of the Urania Trust and a Director of the Alexandria I-Base project. She offers a free monthly newsletter service now in its eighth year.

Exploring the Financial Universe

The Role of the Sun and Planets in the World of Finance Activity

CHRISTEEN H. SKINNER

• A view of the correlation between planetary cycles and financial markets
• The author is well respected and active in the field of Financial Astrology

The role of the Sun, planets and stars and their influence on global markets is intriguing to traders and investors alike. Christeen Skinner's research shows very definite links between major stock market movements and the position of the planets. This book will be of interest to those with little understanding of astrology as well as to those well-versed in the subject. The work includes charts, graphs and horoscopes and explanation of some of the techniques used for astro-financial forecasting.

This book covers solar rhythms and the intricacies of commodity, property and currency price movements with planet cycles. The role of the planets in mastering the relationship between time and price is considered. There is chapter on the natal horoscope and financial rhythms set from birth. The book concludes with forecasts covering 2017–2024.

The author presents case studies in business astrology and an explanation of some astro-finance trading techniques.

Illustrated with financial charts taken from the Optuma software program for astro-traders.

$22.95 • ISBN: 978-089254-218-5
Ebook: 978-089254-632-9
Paperback • 6 x 9 • 224 pages • Illustrated

The Beginners Guide to the Financial Universe

An Introduction to the Role of the Sun, Moon, and Planets in Financial Markets

CHRISTEEN H. SKINNER

- An absolutely necessary guide to succeeding in this turbulent investment climate.
- For market traders curious to know if there is indeed a correlation between happenings in the solar system and market moves.
- For astrologers, a glimpse into the interaction between the planets and commodities and index trading.

Written in response to demand from clients and astrology students, this book provides an introduction to the the role of the Sun, Moon, planets and major planet cycles in the market.

This book takes a step by step approach to understanding the effect of events in the solar system and market movements. Starting with the sunspot cycle, moving on to seasonality charts and lunar trading, the author presents information in an easy to read style. As viewed from Earth, the planets each have periods when they appear retrograde i.e. moving backward relative to Earth. These periods and their correlation with market activity are considered as is the role of Mars. There is a recognized twenty year business cycle: the exact period between one conjunction of Jupiter and Saturn and the next. The phases of this cycle are explored. The concluding chapter offers date, time and place data that can be used for further investigation.

Illustrated with financial charts taken from the Optuma software program for astro-traders.

$24.95 • ISBN: 978-089254-224-6
Ebook: 978-089254-640-4
Paperback • 8.5 x 11 • 208 pages • Illustrated